SIX LECTURES

ON THE

ARK OF THE COVENANT.

SIX LECTURES

ON THE

ARK OF THE COVENANT

BY THE

REV. W. H. HAVERGAL, M.A.,

HONORARY CANON OF WORCESTER, AND

INCUMBENT OF SHARESHILL.

LONDON:

HAMILTON, ADAMS, AND CO.,

MDCCCLXVII.

G. WILLIAMS AND CO, PRINTERS, WOLVERHAMPTON.

PREFATORY NOTE.

THESE Lectures were preached, during the Lent of 1852, in the parish Church of St. Nicholas, Worcester, of which the author was then the Rector.

From that time to the present they have lain untouched, and, consequently, have had a longer sleep than the prescribed literary period.

They have at length been awakened by the kind proposal of a once attentive and grateful hearer, still resident in Worcester. That proposal exempts the author from all risk of loss in their publication.

When the Lectures were preached, many passages were extemporaneously supplemented by practical remarks, which are not now attempted to be supplied. No apology is offered for disregarding the hard and stringent rule of which the late Bishop Marsh was the chief exponent in England, namely, that nothing in the Old Testament is to be considered *typical* unless recognised as such in the New Testament. The opponents of the rule might be mustered into a splendid host, among whom should be reckoned one who seems to have been forgotten, namely, the writer of the homily for Whitsunday.

Should the publication of the present Lectures prove acceptable as a means of spiritual edification, others of a similar character may follow; e.g., on " Job," " Melchisedeck," " The Passover," The " Last Words of David," " The Queen of Sheba," " Gethsemane," &c., &c., &c.

Any profits which may accrue will be devoted towards the erection of a Parsonage House, in the parish of Pipe and Lyde, near Hereford.

Want of sight disables the author from any inspection of either manuscripts or proofs. For this service he is indebted to his kind friend and former helper in the parish of St. Nicholas, the Rev. S. B. James.

PYRMONT, N. W. GERMANY,
    August, 1867.

CONTENTS.

—

	PAGE.
The history of the Ark of the Covenant under Moses	1
Its typical reference to Christ	17
Its history under Joshua	33
Its history under the Judges	50
Its history under David and Solomon	68
Its history from the reign of Solomon to the last authentic mention of it	86

THE ARK OF THE COVENANT.

LECTURE I.

"The ark of the covenant overlaid round about with gold, wherein was the golden pot that had manna, and Aaron's rod that budded, and the tables of the covenant; and over it the cherubims of glory shadowing the mercy-seat."—Hebrews ix. 4, 5.

THE inspired Apostle, in this part of his epistle, commences a brief description of the ancient Tabernacle and its glorious furniture. Neither the one nor the other were extant in his day; for the tabernacle had been superseded by the temple, and that temple, with the principal articles which adorned it, had been either plundered or destroyed. But, the revelation of what had been was intensely interesting to every Jew. To the Apostle, however, they were more than interesting. They were to his mental eye luminous and invaluable types of either the Saviour or his Gospel. He, therefore, felt a double interest in explaining them to his "kinsmen according to the flesh:" for, it can hardly be doubted that, in some of his many discourses to the Hebrews, he followed out the object of this brief epistle, and largely expounded the evangelical intention of

B

both the furniture and the services of the tabernacle, to which they too commonly attached a carnal meaning.

Fully assured, then, that the record of Jewish rites, and of everything indeed, which pertained to the tabernacle is preserved for Gentile instruction, and that the very soul and spirit of Christianity is contained in them, we cannot do otherwise than well, if, at the present season, we commence a series of lectures respecting that most glorious and most venerable symbol, "The Ark of the Covenant." That symbol was the very heart and core of the Mosaic system. Every service had reference to it. The prosperity of the nation was intimately connected with it: and the history of many ages received its character from it. As a theological subject, therefore, "the ark of the covenant" is beautifully diffuse in itself, and pleasantly inviting to the biblical student. May our contemplation of it be abundantly profitable, and largely sanctified by the Holy Spirit!

I. The Apostle speaks of " the ark of the covenant" as a thing well known to the Hebrews. But it was known to them only as described by report and the written Word of God. For full four hundred years it had been lost to the Jewish nation. Consequently, neither the writer nor any reader of this epistle had ever seen it. Now, as Jewish report was of very uncertain accuracy; but, as the divine record is as full and as authentic to us as it was to them, we are as competent as the Hebrews themselves to form correct ideas of what the ark really was, and for what purposes it was designed.

1. The word ark, though applied, in the English tongue, to the vessel which Noah built, to the bulrush basket or

fabric in which the babe Moses was concealed, and the coffer or chest in which the tables of the law were deposited, is not one and the same word in the Hebrew language. The ark of Noah, and the little ark of the Nile, were each "*Thebat*": whereas the ark of the covenant was "*Arun.*"

2. This ark of the covenant, independently of "the mercy-seat" above it, was simply a chest or coffer, made of cedar wood and gold plates, but wrought with the most exquisite workmanship.

3. The dimensions of it were not at all considerable, nor so large as is popularly supposed, especially as four Levites were appointed to bear it. According to ordinary computation it was only three feet nine inches long, two feet three inches broad, and two feet three inches deep. But, it was fitted for the purpose for which Jehovah designed it: and he, in all his designs, is eminently observable for consulting fitness of operation for the end in view. There is nothing superfluous in any of his works. They are neither too large nor too little; but admirably fitted for their respective ends. Hence, as this ark or chest was intended as a case to contain the tables of the Law, we can pretty well ascertain the size of these tables. Certainly, they were not half so large as some of those tall "Tables of Commandments" which garnish many a chancel of our country churches. They could not have been more than three feet six inches long and two feet wide, being, in fact, like a pair of large folding slates, or thin stone tablets, such as Moses, or any man, might conveniently carry on one arm, when walking up a hill. There were, however,

other purposes to be answered by this ark, besides this one
of containing the tablets of the testimony. We shall see
what they were, when we have seen a little further into the
structure of the ark itself.

4. When God gave directions to Moses for building the
tabernacle of worship, the first thing which He described,
and the first which He ordered to be made was this ark of
the covenant. The details of its formation are set down in
Exodus xxv. 10—16.

" And they shall make an ark of shittim wood : two cubits and a
half shall be the length thereof and a cubit and a half the breadth
thereof, and a cubit and a half the height thereof.

" And thou shalt overlay it with pure gold; within and without
shalt thou overlay it, and shall make upon it a crown of gold round
about.

" And thou shalt make staves of shittim wood, and overlay them
with pure gold.

" And thou shalt put the staves into the rings by the sides of the
ark, that the ark may be borne by them.

" The staves shall be in the rings of the ark : they shall not be taken
from it.

" And thou shalt put into the ark the testimony which I shall give
thee."

We here find certain particulars which require attentive
observation :

(1.) God Himself is the architect of the ark. Everything respecting it originates with Him. He, also, as a
subsequent chapter discloses to us, inspires an artist for the
fulfilment of the design : so, as the artist wrought under
His inspiration, the workmanship of the ark was truly
divine. In Exodus xxxi. 1—7, we read what is recorded
on this point.

" And the Lord spake unto Moses, saying,

" See, I have called by name Bezaleel, the son of Uri, the son of Hur, of the tribe of Judah:

" And I have filled him with the spirit of God, in wisdom, and in understanding, and in knowledge, and in all manner of workmanship,

" To devise cunning works, to work in gold, and in silver, and in brass,

"And in cutting of stones, to set them, and in carving of timber, to work in all manner of workmanship.

" And I, behold, I have given with him Aholiab, the son of Ahisamach, of the tribe of Dan: and in the hearts of all that are wise-hearted I have put wisdom, that they may make all that I have commanded thee ;

" The tabernacle of the congregation, and the ark of the testimony, and the mercy-seat that is thereupon, and all the furniture of the tabernacle."

In the thirty-seventh chapter and first verse, we are expressly certified that it was Bezaleel who made the ark.

(2.) The materials of the ark were of the most choice and costly kind, and yet they were, in reality, only two. They were fragrant cedar wood and pure gold. The wood formed the shell of the chest, and the gold overlaid every part of it, both within and without.

(3.) Round the topmost edges of the sacred chest was a projecting rim of gold, called "a crown, or coronet of gold round about." This, though called a crown, was not a lid or cover, (for that was a very different thing, as we have presently to see,) but it was a sort of fence or border, parallel with the outside edge, ornamentally formed like a coronet, and intended to fit the mercy seat, which was put on like a lid or cover upon the topmost edges of the ark.

(4.) On each of the four corners of the ark, Bezaleel was

to put a ring of cast gold—to form sockets for the insertion of staves, by which the Levites might bear it on their shoulders. The four rings and the four bearers would necessarily be in four different places; which might be intended for an intimation to the Jews, that the True Ark should eventually be carried to the four quarters of the world.

(5.) The staves, by which the ark was borne, were of precisely the same materials as the ark itself. They were to be of shittim wood or cedar, overlaid with gold. One remarkable injunction was given respecting them, viz.: that, when once put in, they were never to be taken out of the rings, for which they were fitted. They were always to remain in readiness for use: and this might be to testify that the Levites ought always to be in readiness to use them; and that the God, whom the ark represented, was ever ready to rise up on behalf of those who were ready to follow Him.

5. The primary intention of the ark was, as you have heard, and as the Jews were often reminded, for containing the tables of the Law, otherwise called the testimony or the covenant. "Thou shalt put into the ark the testimony which I will give thee."

The ten commandments were a summary of God's mind to man. They described, in brief, all that He required of man. They were the ground of a covenant between Him and the people; and, inasmuch as they were written on two tablets, those tablets were the testimonies of the covenant, because they at once testified God's will to the people, and would testify against the people if they failed to keep them. Hence, as God's law or testimony was everything to God, we read of "the tables of the testimony" (Exodus xxxi. 18), and "the ark of the testimony" (Exodus xxv. 22), and "the tabernacle of the testimony" (Exodus xxxviii. 21). In after times, the term "testimony" was applied to the whole book of the law, and now it is applied to the gospel also.

But, strange to say, when God directed the ark to be made for holding the tables of the law, those tables were not in existence. The Law itself had been given, but the tables, on which it was written, were not yet entrusted to Moses. So provident is the God of providence. He makes due preparation for everything, especially for the preservation of the things which are dearest to Him. He prepared paradise for Adam before he formed Adam himself. He planned Noah's ark long before Noah was in danger. And now He gives directions for a receptacle for the testimony before that testimony is inscribed on the tables of stone. So, also, (and glory be to His holy name for it!) when He gave the law, which He knew the people would break, He had well provided a mediator and substitute who should perfectly keep it. In the fulness of time, Christ was made under the law, that He might redeem those who were in bondage to the curse of it.

II. In our text, as usually read, it is asserted that, besides "the tables of the covenant," the pot of manna and Aaron's rod that budded were *in* the ark.

"The ark of the covenant overlaid round about with gold, wherein was the golden pot that had manna, and Aaron's rod that budded, and the tables of the covenant;

"And over it the cherubims of glory shadowing the mercy seat; of which we cannot now speak particularly."

As this apparent assertion is in direct opposition to 1 Kings VIII. 9, it is proper that the seeming contradiction should be set right. That verse, with emphatic precision, declares that "There was *nothing in the ark save the two tables of stone*, which Moses put there at Horeb."

Added to this declaration is the fact that nowhere in the Old Testament is it said that the pot of manna and Aaron's rod were *in* the ark. On the contrary, it is constantly stated that they were *before* the ark, i.e., by it, near it, in presence of it, within the veil, together with the few other things which were permitted to have a place in the holy of holies. (Exodus XVI. 33, 34. Numbers XVII. 10.)

Learned men have spent, perhaps wasted, much time in devising ingenious methods of reconciling the apparent contradiction.* Their pains, as Bishop Patrick has observed, might have been spared by a very simple, but very truthful process: for the two Greek terms in our text, translated by one word "wherein," may as properly, and do as commonly mean by which, with which, or near † which, as in which or "wherein." A multitude of quotations could be speedily adduced to prove the fact of such meaning of the terms. There is, therefore, no real diffi-

---

* "Andrew Sennertus, of Wittemberg, (circ. 1655) compiled a work which contained nearly everything which had been surmised upon the subject."

† "*In* the place where He was crucified (meaning, evidently, *near* to the place) was a garden."—John xix. 41.

culty in the case—particularly to those who have a due knowledge of the original tongues.

To justify our translation, however, it has been suggested that the word "wherein" refers not to "the ark of the covenant," but to the holy of holies, in which the ark itself was. The passage must then be read in this manner : "And after the second veil, the tabernacle, which is called "the holiest of all; which had the golden censer and the "ark of the covenant, overlaid round about with gold; "wherein (i.e., in which tabernacle) was the golden pot that "had manna, and Aaron's rod that budded, and the tables "of the covenant." The original Greek may bear this sense, but it is with a strain. The far easier and preferable method is the one already suggested. In corroboration, also, of the pretty plain fact that there was nothing really in the ark but the tables of the law, let it be borne in mind that, if the ark itself was only three feet six inches long, it would be far too short to contain a rod which, in all probability, was nearly double that length.

The supposed discrepancy is just one of those occurrences which should arm humble readers of the bible against the cavils of infidel objectors; and, at the same time, make them confident in the integrity of Holy Scripture, and thankful for its abundant plainness.

It is proper for it further to be noticed that, in the text, we are told a little additional fact, which is not mentioned in the Old Testament. The pot which contained the manna is described as a "*golden* pot." This is not told us by Moses. But, that a pot or vessel, used for the storing of manna, should be made of gold, is both very likely in itself and quite in keeping with all that surrounded it. Gold was truly fitting for the formation of a vessel which was to hold a miraculous product, and the very preservation of which was itself a standing miracle. The manna, when originally given, would only keep for a single day, or, at the most, for two days, when the second day was the Sabbath. But, when deposited in the golden pot before the ark it was perpetually preserved from putrefaction, and became a type of that "hidden manna" which ever liveth in the true holy of holies for the vital sustenance of the spiritual nation below.

III. Appended to the ark, and, in one sense, part and parcel of it, was the mercy-seat, with the cherubim of glory over it. "And over it the cherubims of glory, shadowing the mercy-seat."

This propitiatory, or mercy-seat, was the grand object of Hebrew awe and solemn veneration. All that was dear to Israel was centred in it, for it was the precise and secret place of the divine presence, as well as being in itself peculiarly significant of great and important truths.

The description of this mercy-seat, and how it was to be made, is recorded in the verses which follow the description of the formation of the ark. (Exodus xxv. 17—22.)

"And thou shalt make a mercy-seat of pure gold: two cubits and a half shall be the length thereof, and a cubit and a half the breadth thereof

"And thou shalt make two cherubims of gold, of beaten work shalt thou make them, in the two ends of the mercy-seat.

"And make one cherub on the one end, and the other cherub on the other end: even of the mercy-seat shall ye make the cherubims on the two ends thereof.

" And the cherubims shall stretch forth their wings on high, covering the mercy-seat with their wings, and their faces shall look one to another; toward the mercy-seat shall the faces of the cherubims be,

" And thou shalt put the mercy-seat above upon the ark; and in the ark thou shalt put the testimony that I shall give thee.

" And there I will meet with thee; and I will commune with thee from above the mercy-seat, from between the two cherubims which are upon the ark of the testimony, of all things which I will give thee in commandment unto the children of Israel."

1. This so-called " mercy-seat " was the lid or covering for the ark, and was made entirely of gold—pure and solid. It was exactly as long and as broad as the ark itself; and so, fitting it closely on the top, was kept in its place by its own weight, and by the golden rim or coronet-like fringe which went all around the edges of the ark, and so, of course, prevented it, when standing or carried evenly, from slipping off. How thick it was is not stated; but certain circumstances induce the belief that it was firm and strong.

2. At each of the two ends of the mercy-seat was a mystical figure, called a cherub. Each was also made of gold, only not fastened *on* to the mercy-seat, but wrought out of the same metallic mass, and so constituting an inseparable part of the mercy-seat itself. This fact of the cherubim and the mercy-seat being beaten, not molten, out of one and the same mass of gold, was peremptorily commanded of God, and punctually observed by Bezaleel. " He made two " cherubims of gold, *beaten out of one piece* made he them " on the two ends of the mercy-seat."

The intention of their being thus formed out of one piece is not clear to us. Doubtless, it was mystical and important, as well as worthy of Him, who will, one day, enable us better to understand it.   Nevertheless, an opinion or two will presently be stated.

3. What was the exact figure, aspect, and meaning of these golden cherubim has been, and perhaps will, on earth, always be a very hard and disputed point.   Various descriptions are given of the cherubim, particularly by Ezekiel ɪ. 4—14, and by St. John in Rev. ɪᴠ. 6, 7, 8, from which it appears that they were "winged beings," with four diverse faces, and one human-like body, terminating in ox or "calf" shaped feet.   But, whether this was their peculiar form on the ark is by no means certain.   Josephus, (Antiq. ɪɪɪ. 6.) when speaking of them, says—with no little point—they " were *winged animals, resembling nothing that was ever seen by men.*"   That they sometimes resembled an ox is certain from what Ezekiel says in chapter x. 14, compared with ɪ. 10, where the face of an ox and the face of a cherub are reckoned one and the same.   And yet *the union* of the man's face with the lion's face is mysteriously significant!   Solomon made, for the holy place in the temple, two very large cherubim of olive-tree wood, whose wings shadowed nearly the whole of the area.   The cherubim on the ark were of comparatively small dimensions.

As to their mystical meaning, the two principal opinions are these: A small, but goodly number of theologians regard them as symbols of the Trinity in Unity; and support their opinion by, at least, very ingenious and very interesting arguments, which, however, are too long and too erudite to be even recapitulated here.   Suffice it to add, that the beating out of the cherubim from the same mass of gold as the mercy-seat, is with them a strong fact for the support of their opinion that those cherubim were symbols of deity and not of angelic existences: because, say they, as the mercy-seat was confessedly emblematical of divine graciousness, so must the cherubic figures be emblems of divine powers, inasmuch as they were formed out of the same metallic mass, which is tantamount to being of the same nature.

The generality of divines take a different (I will not say a more satisfactory) view of the case. They consider these figures as intended to represent the persons and services of angels, who derive their being from God, are partakers of his holy nature, and are not only intensely interested in the grant of mercy to fallen man, but are zealously employed in carrying it out.

The turning of their faces downwards and inwards towards each other is taken for a sign of their reverent humility, their deep earnestness respecting God's law and God's mercy to the transgressors of it, and their own perfect agreement with, and inclination towards, one another· The outstretching and overshadowing of their wings are thought to represent their constant readiness to fly anywhere for the execution of God's commands, and their attendance around his seat of glory in heaven.

4. Be these things as they may, we are sure of one thing, which is the great thing of the whole, that the mercy-seat, when placed on the ark, was, to the Jews, the visible throne of the invisible God.—(Exodus xxv. 22.) Here, on the mercy-seat, dwelt the Shechinah, or glorious ray of the divine presence. Before it all Israel trembled. In front stood the high priest once a year, when making a ritual

atonement for the sins of the people. And, from it, came forth the voice of Jehovah, when Moses, or any other appointed mediator, consulted the God of the nation.

5. When the tabernacle and all its furniture were completed, a day was fixed for the setting up of the whole in due order. On the first day of the first month of the second year of Israel's entrance in the wilderness, the entire fabric was erected on its dry and burning sands. It must have been a deeply interesting moment in the life of Moses when, with his own hands, he took the two tables of the law, and devoutly placed them within the ark; for that he so did, and that he also put the mercy-seat upon the ark, we are expressly told in Exodus xI. 20.

After this, and during the life-time of Moses, no particular incident seems to have occurred to the ark beyond the ordinary occurrences which were previously arranged respecting it. When the time came for the tribes to leave their encampment at Horeb, the tabernacle was taken down, and the ark was carried forward, in the manner prescribed, to be at once a guide and a defence. An interesting description of what was done and said is given in Numbers x. 33—36. Regarding it then as thoroughly perfect, and placed in its destined position within the veil, let us give a retrospective glance upon it, and what concerns it.

1. View the ark as possessing this remarkable peculiarity. *It was not only the first thing made for the tabernacle, but the chief thing for which the tabernacle itself was made.* It was to the whole Jewish system what the heart is to animal economy. The heart is the first thing formed in man, or

beast, or bird; and, to each, it is essential to vitality. Keep the heart in sound and healthy action, and all is well. Take the heart away, and all is gone. So was it with "the ark of the covenant." It was made before the other vessels of the sanctuary, or even the sanctuary itself was made. All was well in Israel when it occupied its proper place as to locality and the affections of the people. But, when it was removed and lost, "the glory departed from Israel," as the dying wife of Phineas too plaintively said. So, afterwards, when the ark was absent from the tabernacle, it was like the absence of Jehovah Himself; for, on that occasion, it is said, (1 Samuel VII. 2) "All the house of Israel lamented after the Lord."

2. View the ark as *a beautifully-instructive symbol to the Jewish nation.* It taught them, in substance, what the gospel teaches us. The tables of the law can be approached only by the *mercy*-seat. Unless that mercy covered over human violations of the law, judgment would come forth to destruction.

It taught the Jews, also, that there was no communion with a holy God, but on the ground of his own mercy. These things would induce inquiring minds to seek further into the truths which respect salvation; and God's good spirit was ever ready to teach them.

3. Seeing, then, that all these circumstances and particulars were divinely prescribed, and have been divinely communicated and preserved, we may be sure of their high importance. For our learning they were written, and God expects us to learn them. We ought, indeed, to read and mark them well, not only on account of their value, but also on account of their extreme interest and profit.

Christians are not universally awake to the benefits of a careful study of Old Testament topics. They are not so interested with them as the Apostles were, for they regarded them as "the lively oracles," and the ancient store-house of saving truth. It will be one object of the present lectures "to stir up pure minds by way of remembrance," and to encourage all to a wider perusal of God's word, and a more pains-taking study of its contents.

LECTURE II.

"Which are a shadow of things to come, but the body is of Christ."
—Colossians ii. 17.

THOUGH St. Paul speaks these words with immediate reference to the meats and drinks, times and seasons of the Jewish church, yet he does not, by any means, confine them to those things. He the rather uses them, as elsewhere, with relation to the whole Jewish ritual. Everything in that ritual, as is again and again stated in the epistle to the Hebrews, was intended to foreshadow and prefigure either the person or the truth of Christ. The law, as therein said, had " a shadow of good things to come ;" and the tabernacle, with *all* its furniture, " was a figure for the time then present."—(Hebrews x. 1, and IX. 9.) Consequently, as the whole includes the parts, and " the law " and " the tabernacle " included " the ark of the covenant," that ark was " a figure " of Christ,—a shadow of the " good things to come " in Him,—a shadow of which the body was Himself. The word " shadow," as used in

c

our text, and in other texts, is variously interpreted. Some
divines construe it in the sense of *an outline* such as a
portrait painter traces before he begins the filling up. This
idea represents everything Mosaic as a mere outline, of
which Christ was to be the full portrait. Others, however,
regard it as the reflection of an object in a mirror, or by
the sun. The shadow only is discerned, but the real object
which it reflects is so placed as not yet to be seen. Consequently, the thing discerned is neither real nor satisfactory.
It does but represent that which the mind desires. Thus,
"the ark of the covenant," though a real object in itself,
was not the real object of Jehovah's intention. It was
only a shadow of Christ. In the former lecture we considered "the ark of the covenant as to its history under
Moses." We are now, according to the plan proposed, to
consider "the ark as to its reference to the Lord Jesus
Christ." As we have to contemplate the subsequent ages
of the ark's historical existence, we shall not anticipate that
history, but confine our view of it to the time when it stood,
in all its completeness, in "the tent of the testimony," when
set up by Moses in the wilderness. It was then a magnificent shadow, of which Christ was the body. But, here,
let me meet an objection which less thoughtful persons are
wont to raise against the study of such shadows, and which,
therefore, applies to a discourse like the present. What
need, say these objectors, is there to concern ourselves about
the old shadows of the law which have long passed away?
Had we not better give our undivided attention to Him,
who is the substance of them all, now that He is clearly
revealed to us? Why not consider Christ directly and at

once—in His manifested person—rather than by looking back to the ark, which has long ago ceased to exist? There is much plausibility in these questions, but there is, also, no little infidelity lurking in them. Our answer to them is this: Though the Mosaic shadows have passed away, the record of them remains. That record is the word of Christ, and is given for our study. If we study it as he explained it, we *must* come to the things of the law; for Himself expounded to the disciples at Emmaus "the things which were written concerning Him *in the law*." When, therefore, we find Christ in the law, that law becomes the gospel to us, and all its incidents and circumstances are only so many interesting delineations of his person and character. In a word, the *figures* of the law are turned into evangelical *memorials*, which are replete with the richest instruction to all who desire to know the fulness of the gospel. There is a remark upon this subject taken by Bishop Horne from the writings of the celebrated Pascal, which is so wise, beautiful, and appropriate, that its introduction here is almost unavoidable. "Under the Jewish economy, truth " appeared but in figure: in heaven it is open and without " a veil: in the church militant it is so veiled *as yet to be* " *discerned by its correspondence with the figure. As the figure* " *was first built up in the truth, so the truth is now distinguish-* " *able by the figure.*"—(Bishop Horne on the Psalms. Preface p. XXI.)

In contemplating "the ark of the covenant" in its relation to Christ, the following arrangement will be observed:—First, the ark itself; next, the mercy-seat as placed on the ark; and then, the uses of the ark and the mercy-seat combined. May the God of the ark show us his mercy, and grant us his grace!

I. *The ark itself in its typical relation to Christ.* Without any such typical relation, it would have been a merely splendid and curious fabric, but nothing more. There would have been nothing glorious, nothing instructive, nothing valuable in it. So true is it that every external object is important, only so far as it refers to Christ.

Let us search for the typical relation of the ark to Him in the following particulars:

1. *The ark was composed of only two substances*—cedar wood and pure gold. Nothing else whatever was used in its structure. Now, as cedar wood is a product of the earth, and gold a settled formation, the one is a fit representation of the earthly nature of Christ, and the other of his heavenly origin. In one person He unites two, and only two, natures, the human and the divine, not at all the angelic. Though man, He was God; and in a manner, too, which was shadowed by the union of cedar and gold in the composition of the ark.

The human nature was taken into union with the divine essence. So the gold covered the cedar wood, embraced and embosomed it, as it were, in such wise as to be one with it, and inseparable from it.

The incorruptibility of our Lord's humanity was, also, foreshadowed by the cedar wood; for it is a proverbially durable wood. Pliny, the classical naturalist, called it "the wood of eternity." Fit emblem, therefore, was it of that body which could "see no corruption." United with the gold it became a noble figure of that union of humanity and deity which are never to be separated. The two natures make but one Christ for ever and ever.

2. *The design of the ark was to contain the tables of the law.* It was built for that express purpose, and called after it accordingly. God's law was both a covenant and a testimony—a covenant between Him and the people, and a testimony of his own mind to them for the regulation of their conduct towards Him. The ark was " the ark of the covenant " or of the testimony, because it was the splendid, stately, and solemn receptacle of the tables or records of it.

These tables were, also, a renewed or second set; the first having been broken in anger for the sin of the people. Now, because Adam broke the divine law, when it was first given to him, it was renewed and placed in better hands than his. It was put within an ark which held it safe till all that it demanded had been fully accomplished. Christ was that ark. His incarnation took place in order that He might embody the perfect law of God, and perfectly keep it for the honour of God and the salvation of man. "Thy law (said He prophetically) is within my heart. I delight to do Thy will, O my God." Because of the safety and inviolable integrity of the law, in the person of Christ, all His believing followers fulfil the law in Him, and are justified by the righteousness of Him who fulfilled it.

3. *The ark was the first thing which was formed for the tabernacle, and that very thing for which the tabernacle and all else was constructed.* Nothing else was named before it. It took the precedence of everything, in both the command for its execution and in the execution itself. How vividly

does this fact testify the priority of Him who is the true ark of the living God! Is not Jesus "the First" of all beings, and of all things! Is He not the first begotten and the first born? Is He not "*before* all things"? And are not " all things made *for* Him "? Yes, verily, He is First and All. Eternity will unfold his priority and pre-eminence to a degree which our poor understandings cannot now comprehend. But, when we see the true tabernacle, we shall see how it all was built for the glory of the true ark.

4. *The ark had a crown-like border all round its topmost edge.* "Thou shalt make upon it a crown of gold round about." So that, although this crown of gold was for a fence, or enveloping border, to hold fast the mercy-seat, yet did it give to the ark a noble, stately, and regal appearance. What could better represent the regal character of Him whom the ark itself represented? Though despised as a Nazarene, He is the "king of saints." " On His head are many crowns." The Father hath set on Him " a crown of pure gold," and He shall wear it when all other crowns are either cast before Him or crumbled into dust. May we acknowledge his beauty, and bow to his authority!

5. *The ark was a work of inspiration.* The Spirit of God came down upon Bezaleel on purpose for the work. Without that inspiration he would have been unequal to the task; and, as to its mystical intention, he never could have even surmised it. The body of our adorable Saviour was, we must ever reverently recollect, the work of inspiration. The Holy Ghost came down on his virgin mother, and He " was *made* man." We are told the fact, and it is essential to our salvation that we believe it. The whole mystery is

super-human. No Bezaleel anticipated it; neither can any unfold it. Curiosity is baffled, but faith is abundantly satisfied. "Great is the mystery of Godliness! God was manifest in the flesh."

6. *The ark, thus constructed, was never to be looked into, nor touched by ordinary persons.* The prying eye and the forward hand were alike prohibited. Death was the penalty for infringing the prohibition. The Hebrews well understood this regulation; and once beheld an affecting proof of its force, when, in after days, Uzzah died, for even his well-intended interference.

This reverence to be observed towards the ark was intended to teach all men that they must honour the Son as they honour the Father. Other types, such as the manna from heaven, and the water from the rock, shewed that Christ was freely to be received, and intimately considered; but this declared that He is, at the same time, to be regarded with the profoundest reverence and the utmost awe. He is the high and lofty one, and His name is holy—so holy that none are to take it in vain, but every knee is to bow down at it.

The type also, in this aspect of it, teaches us to abstain from vain speculation, curious inquiry, and even mere philosophical investigation, respecting those things pertaining to the nature and person of Christ, which are "secret to us."

From this part of our subject let us proceed to contemplate

II. *The mercy-seat as placed on the ark.* The mercy-seat, or throne of propitiation, though considered part and parcel of the ark, was yet, in its structure, perfectly distinct from it. A distinct command was given respecting it. A distinct notice is taken of its formation : and a very precise account is recorded of the act of Moses in placing it on the ark.

Bearing in mind what was said of it in the former lecture, let us search out its typical reference to Jesus the Lord.

1. Being ALL of gold *it represented the Godhead; and being set on the ark it declared the oneness of that Godhead with Christ as the Incarnate Son.* At the baptism of the beloved Son, the Father audibly acknowledged and honoured Him, and the Eternal Spirit came down visibly and bodily upon Him. Indeed, Holy Scripture labours, as it were, to show us that the Father honours the Son, sets his seal upon Him, and rests in his love for Him. The oneness of the Father and the Son was a frequent topic of discourse with our Lord Himself. "I and my Father are one," was that saying which the ark had long whispered to Israel, before Jesus declared it aloud.

2. The mercy-seat was emphatically " *the propitiatory*," or *the token of the mercy of God to all penitent transgressors of the law.* It was so shaped as to resemble a seat or throne ; and Jehovah was pleased to make it his visible throne of grace and mercy. But, being placed over the tables of the law in the ark, it betokened, to every thoughtful Israelite, the grant of mercy to the transgressors of that law, only through a covering or propitiation for their transgressions. Hence it was a clear and intelligible type of Him " whom God hath set forth to be a propitiation for

sin, through faith in his blood." He covered the law which was against us—shut up its curses and hushed its thunders—by virtue of that mercy which was like a solid and an impenetrable lid to the ark which contained them. Well might the beloved disciple, when an aged apostle, delight to say (1 John II. 2, and IV. 10.)

" And he is the propitiation for our sins: and not for ours only, but also for the sins of the whole world."

" Herein is love, not that we loved God, but that he loved us, and sent his Son to be the propitiation for our sins."

3. From the mercy-seat *God shone forth* in a manner which declared his presence to Israel. So far as we can understand the case, it appears that on the day of the erection of the tabernacle in the wilderness, a luminous cloud descended upon "the tent of the testimony," and that a portion of it took its station between the cherubim on the mercy-seat. The Jews called this bright but softened light the Shekinah; and, in their Rabbinical writings, say much respecting it.

But, this light on the mercy-seat, which marked the certainty of the divine presence, was but a type of "the true light," even of Christ, who declared Himself to be such. He is the manifestation of Deity, "the brightness of the Father's glory," and the only visible image of the God who is light. But, more on this subject, under another division of it.

4. *On the mercy-seat God received supplications, and from it gave answers to questions.* When any went to unburthen their hearts, or seek directions, under the pressure of calamities or perplexities, it was before the ark that they

fell down. Suppliants and inquirers were sure to meet
with the omnipotent and omniscient Jehovah on his mercy-
seat. It was both an oratory and an oracle of the living
God for faithful Israelites. What the ark was, in these
respects, to them, the Lord Jesus now is to us. He is the
only channel of prayer to God, and the only medium of
communication from God. Through Him alone God hears
us, and speaks to us. "No man cometh unto the Father,
but by Him." He, too, is the only "word" of the
Father; for the Father's voice sounds to us through Him.
Hence all Holy Scripture, though called the word of God,
is also called "the word of Christ." In Numbers VII. 89,
it is said,

"When Moses was gone into the tabernacle of the congregation to
speak with Him, then he heard the voice of one speaking unto him
from off the mercy-seat that was upon the ark of testimony, from
between the two cherubims."

This "speaking from off the mercy-seat" was the type of
God's speaking to his people through Christ: for —
Hebrews I. 1, 2,

"God who at sundry times and in divers manners spake in times
past unto the fathers by the prophets

"Hath in these last days spoken unto us by his Son, whom he hath
appointed heir of all things, by whom also he made the worlds."

5. If the cherubim, on the ends of the mercy-seat,
represented the angelic hosts, then are we to understand
that *it is only through the mediation of Christ that angels
minister unto us.* Without a propitiation for our sins, there
would have been no pathway from heaven to our world.
But, because there is a great propitiation for us in Christ,
there is angelic access to us at his bidding. Jacob saw it

in the vision of the ladder; and the Lord Jesus expounded its meaning when he said to Nathaniel—John i. 51—

"Verily, verily, I say unto you, hereafter ye shall see heaven open, and the angels of God ascending and descending upon the Son of Man."

We pass on to consider

III. *The uses of the ark and the mercy-seat combined.* Not that they were ever, in reality, disjoined; for neither was the ark complete without the mercy-seat, nor the mercy-seat without the ark. They were only spoken of separately for the clearer discernment of their purposes. So God the Father and God the Holy Ghost are never disjoined from God the Son, except in language for the better perception of their respective offices.

Considering, then, the ark and the mercy-seat as one, we may consider its uses, thus:

1. *It was the visible guarantee of Jehovah's dwelling with Israel.* It proved to the nation that God was not a great way off, but nigh unto them, and in the midst of them. And is not this the very purpose for which Christ became man? Was He not expressly called "Emmanuel" that we might be assured of God's *being with us?* He was; and all the true followers of the Lord Jesus rejoice in his explicit promise—"Lo, *I am with you always,* even unto the end of the world." The Jews saw the ark, and, so, virtually saw God. Jesus said—"He that hath seen Me hath seen the Father also." "I am in the Father, and the Father in Me." Christ on earth was God come down from heaven. He was the "tabernacle of God with man."

2. The ark and the mercy-seat were, at once, *the glory, the guide, and the defence of Israel.* A cloud by day, and a lamp of fire by night, hung over the tent which covered it. It was taken up, at God's bidding, to find a place of encampment for the people ; and no enemy dared to dispute its march. Invisible death was planted around it.

Such is Christ to his church. He is its glory, its guide, its defence. He is a glory within, and "a wall of fire round about." Only let his people trust themselves in his hands, and they will never take a wrong path, never fall into sin, never run into any kind of danger.

3. The ark and the mercy-seat *concentrated the affection, reverence, and contemplation of the people.* It was their rallying point; their visible "all-in-all." It was to them, in reality, what the idol image of Minerva was to the Trojans in mere vain imagination. So long as that image was in their towering citadel, so long they had something on which to repose their admiration and their confidence. It was their "palladium," and so their boast and their joy.

All this and more than this is Christ to his true Israel. So long as He is in the soul of a believer, that believer is conscious of having a supreme object for his affections, and an adorable presence which commands his awe, and brings him peace. Possessing the ark of Christ's presence, we never want a theme for meditation, or a power to cheer and preserve amidst the hot riot of corruptions within, or the embattled assaults of Satan from without. Israel is safe and prosperous while the ark is with them, and God is in all their hearts.

4. *The ark and the mercy-seat were not commonly seen by the people, but only occasionally.* It was covered by a tent without, and concealed by a veil within. Still, the indications of its presence were always clear and decided. Its staves, were, at least, so placed as to be visible, according to some interpreters, to the assembled worshippers. While in the wilderness, as we now are contemplating it, the cloud by day and the fire by night were the incessant index to it. In these circumstances we behold an intimation of the fact that, under the law, Christ was but partially revealed and dimly discerned. As St. Paul says, "The way into the holiest of all was not yet made manifest." The veil was not rent. God was not "manifest in the flesh." Christ was not yet made man. All, therefore, was seen in a sort of faint light—dim and hazy. Occasionally, indeed, the Lord Jesus anticipated his incarnation, and appeared in human form : but that was not the true manifestation of Himself. It was not till angels chanted his birth at Bethlehem that the manhood was revealed to long-expecting eyes. Now that He was come down to us, as bone of our bone and flesh of our flesh, made like unto us in all things, we may see as well as believe.

5. The ark, with the mercy-seat upon it, *had rings and staves for its carriage from place to place.* The whole was, therefore, moveable, and not necessarily restricted to one locality. A glorious truth, and yet a fearful warning, was hereby indicated to the people. The bearing of the ark by four priests, or Levites, seemed to betoken the carrying of the gospel of Christ, recorded by four evangelists, to the four points of the earth. The true ark has long travelled

far beyond the coasts of Judea, and is in progress towards
every corner of the globe. But, the moveable nature of
the ark warns us of the *removeable* nature of the gospel. If
a people despise it, or make light of it, the God of it will
order it to be carried elsewhere. Woe to that nation, city,
town, or village, which has enjoyed the bright presence of
the gospel ark, but through unbelief and negligence has
lost it! No greater scourge can be inflicted on a people,
whether many or few, than the withdrawal of the ark of
Christ's gospel from among them. May God avert such a
calamity from our country, our city, our parish.

And, now, having stated to you wherein " the ark of
the covenant" typically represented the Lord Jesus Christ,
suffer me to remind you of one or two counterfeit representations. That ark was indeed, a type of Christ, but *it
was not a type of his virgin mother.* Roman Catholic books
of devotion abound with blasphemous applications of the
ark to the virgin Mary. They call *her* "the ark of mercy,"
and even "the ark of the covenant," as well as the em-
bodiment of other virtues or perfections, of which the ark
can be considered the receptacle. We know no such
unhallowed touchings of the ark. May God save deluded
votaries from the consequences.

Further, in the path of counterfeit, Roman Catholic
preachers and orators have a fond practice of insinuating
that the ark in the tabernacle was a type of *the pix*, as it is
called, on their altar. The pix is the little coffer, chest, or
box, in which the consecrated host or wafer is kept, and
which is always deposited, as the very body of Christ, on the
high altar; and, therefore, to be bowed to, worshipped,

and adored by every person who turns towards it. In earlier centuries, as Shakespeare pleasantly testifies, "If a man stole a pix, he was to be hanged outright for the theft." We know no such profanation of scripture types, but account them wicked fables and abominable impostures "to be abhorred of all faithful men."

There are many things connected with the ark which are full of pleasant or profitable meditation:

1. We behold, in the ark of the covenant, *a centre of unity between the old testament church and the new testament church.* The true ark of each is the same; for Christ was theirs as well as ours. Dim as the old dispensation certainly was, there was enough light in it for all general purposes: while particular individuals, as our sagest saints believe, were favoured with clearer powers of perception, and saw much of Him whose types were constantly before them. Thus, then, it is pleasant to reflect on the oneness of the faith, and hope, and love of true christians in all ages. Some divines are of opinion that the two cherubim, on the mercy-seat, were symbols of the two churches—the Jewish and the Gentile—united in one mediator of mercy. Be this as it may, we know that all is one in Christ now; and that true believers of every age and clime find the same mediator on one and the same mercy-seat.

2. We behold, in the main features of the ark, *all our desire, and all our salvation.* We see Jesus displayed as the keeper of the law for us, and as the medium of mercy to us. The law is under his mediatorial throne, kept in its own perfect sanctity, and that sanctity forms a basis for his throne. To this blessed Jesus, as the fulfiller of the law

for us, we must come for pardon and righteousness. We have only to approach Him with lively faith, and He will be a lively mediator for us; because, as his seat is all of pure gold, He is the dispenser of golden mercy. The riches of his grace are lavished on us, if we will but gather them up.

3. In the staves of the ark we discern *a joyous token for all lands*. The ark which, after the death of Moses, was borne in triumphant march to a rich but heathen country, symbolized, by its staves, the ultimate intention of its Divine Author respecting the true ark of the new covenant. In due time our ark shall be carried to every pagan clime. Its staves shall always be in its rings, and the feet of its bearers shall be beautiful on all mountains and high hills. May our hearts be a receptacle for it now.

LECTURE III.

"And all Israel and their elders and officers and their judges stood on this side the ark, and on that side, before the priests the Levites, which bare the ark of the covenant of the Lord, as well the stranger as he that was born among them."—Joshua viii. 33.

"THE ark of the covenant of the Lord" was now in the Land of Canaan. It had been brought thither by Joshua, who, after the death of Moses, succeeded to the lofty duties of the government of Israel.

There were four remarkable events, during the age of Joshua, in connection with which the ark is mentioned. Our text has reference to the last of the four. They were —The passage of the Jordan; the marching round Jericho; the defeat of Israel at Ai; and the division of all the tribes —half on Mount Ebal, and half on Mount Gerizim.

Our former lecture was devoted to the consideration of the typical reference of the ark to the Lord Jesus Christ, when, on its completion under Moses, it beautified the tabernacle in the wilderness. You are now invited to contemplate the ark in its history under Joshua; which portion of its history embraces some of the grandest and most marvellous events, whose bare record ever arrested human ears. We cannot, of

D

course, investigate every particular incident in those events, but only such as immediately depend on the presence of the ark.

I. *The passage of the Jordan* is detailed in the third and fourth chapters of this book. The record of it is of that character which indicates that the inspired writer was peculiarly interested with his subject. He minutely states its facts, recurs to them, and lingers on the ground of them as one whose soul was filled with admiration and delight in the recollection of them.

1. Between the passage of the Red Sea and that of the Jordan a very remarkable difference was ordained. When the Israelites crossed a narrow part of the Red Sea, their passage was effected in haste, in the night, and without any notable preparation. The people were driven to a strait; their hearts were faint, and no particular information was given to them as to the mode of their deliverance. Whereas, when the Israelites were about to cross the Jordan, the most deliberate measures were taken, and the calmest preparation was made. The time selected was in that part of the year when the stream of the river was at its broadest and fullest. Messengers were sent through the host to acquaint every man of what was about to be done; and all was done under the brightest beam of day. Instead, too, of the enemies of Israel being behind them, they were full in front of them, and from their walls and watch-towers discerned every movement of their body. "The people passed over right against Jericho."—(Joshua III. 16.) There probably was a typical intention in these remarkable differences. The crossing of the Red Sea is commonly

regarded as analogous to christian Baptism; and the crossing of the Jordan as emblematical of the transit of a believer, by death, into the heavenly Canaan. Now, for baptism, the young Israelite can hardly be said to make preparation. It is prepared for him, rather than he is prepared for it. He is taken through, it may be under a cloud, and with many surrounding pressures. But, when the harnessed and well-travelled believer comes to the end of his journey, he is usually allowed time to prepare for what awaits him. His passage across the full river is often preceded by kindly monitions from his Great Captain; and a bright light and a calm demeanour are vouchsafed to him. May such be our blessed lot when the hour of our departure shall be signified to us!

2. In the passage of the Jordan, the first and last object of universal attention was "the ark of the covenant of the Lord." Every eye was to be directed to it, and every movement regulated by it.

Ordinarily, the Levites were the bearers of it; but, upon this grand and solemn occasion, certain priests were selected for the memorable task. It was an honour to them, and they reverently undertook it.

And, now, their task commences. They bear up the ark as soon as Israel have taken down their tents, and are ready to march. And, as they apply their shoulders to the staves, a hallowed awe fills their breasts; because they know that "the Lord of all the earth," as Himself said to Joshua, was concentrating Himself "on the mercy-seat," between the cherubim, in order to guarantee a clear and safe passage to the youngest and feeblest Israelite.

But, the priestly bearers of the awful and precious symbol must themselves begin the passage by an act of faith. They must not only approach the stream, but actually set their feet in it—(Joshua III. 13). They must believe that, on so doing, the waters would be instantly parted to form a passage for the people. So true and fitting is it that they who bear "the ark of the sanctuary," must be the first to exercise faith in the God of it. The ministers of Christ are to be firm believers in his promises, and their faith is to be visible to all men; otherwise, they are not warranted to expect salvation for themselves, or their people. In all difficult and dangerous times, also, they are to head their people, and lead them on in the path of God's ordaining.

Never did Jehovah fail, and never will He fail, to fulfil his word, when obedience is paid to it. Accordingly, we read—(Joshua III. 14—16)

" And it came to pass, when the people removed from their tents, to pass over Jordan, and the priests bearing the ark of the covenant before the people;

" And as they that bare the ark were come unto Jordan, and the feet of the priests that bare the ark were dipped in the brim of the water, (for Jordan overfloweth all his banks all the time of harvest,)

" That the waters which came down from above stood and rose up upon a heap very far from the city Adam, that is beside Zaretan, and those that came down towards the sea of the plain, even the Salt Sea, failed, and were cut off: and the people passed over right against Jericho."

Thus the miracle was as instantaneous as it was stupendous.

The setting of the feet of the priests in the outer edge of the stream was like the instant gash of a mighty sabre-stroke, or the lightning-like fall of a crystal sluice-gate. Quickly as an eye-lid twinkles were the waters from above cut off, in a straight, wall-like line, from those which were below. And, what is so wondrously strange, the waters, instead of spreading out at the sides, piled up, as it were, in a heap, increasing every moment, like a glassy wall built up higher and higher by invisible hands. Jehovah could as speedily have congealed the river, and so have formed a path of ice across it for his people: but this would have borne some resemblance to an operation of nature; it would have been like merely bringing down a stream of the north into a channel of the south. This would have been a miracle, but not such a miracle as the one which had no parallel in nature to represent it.

And, now, on the bed of the Jordan becoming dry, the priests advance with the ark into the very midst of it. They take their stand as men who had nothing to fear from the towering flood above them, because the Maker and Master of all was on the ark which rested on their shoulders, They move not till all had passed over—clean, safe, and triumphant.* Beautiful pledge this of the presence of Christ in the river of death, when his people are passing through it! And sure token is it that He will not depart, and that not one of them shall fail of reaching the celestial shore!

3. But, though "all the people were passed clean over

---

* "And the priests that bare the ark of the covenant of the Lord stood firm on dry ground in the midst of Jordan, and all the Israelites passed over on dry ground, until all the people were passed clean over Jordan."—Joshua iii. 17.

Jordan," the ark does not yet remove. Something more is yet to be done. God gives command through Joshua for twelve picked men — "out of every tribe a man"—to "pass over before the ark" into the midst of Jordan, and to take from thence as large a stone as each could find, to carry to the spot where the ark should lodge that night, after it was brought out of the bed of the river. Of these stones a pile was to be formed "for a memorial to future generations.—(Joshua IV. 6, 7.)

More than this, twelve other stones were gathered, and piled up in the bed of the stream, on the very spot where the priests stood while bearing the ark. And God so modified the force of the returning torrent as not to suffer it to wash them away. Many a boatman, and many a bather, saw them for at least many years after they were there deposited; for it is said, by the writer of this Book, "And they are there unto this day."

4. Thus gloriously and memorably did Jehovah, by his ark, lead his people across the bed of a deep and rapid river. And, doubtless, in the day when his last faithful one shall walk dry-shod through a more formidable river, and find, as all his fellows in the faith have found, that the waters have not only not overflown him, but have not even touched him, then will there be such memorials of the event as infinite wisdom will appoint. It cannot but be that every saved believer will vividly recollect the hour of his passage into eternity. He may have appeared to others insensible of what was passing : but the hidden and immortal principle has been awake and watching every incident, especially the presence of the ark as the glory, security, and comfort of the whole.

And now, after due religious celebrations, and further tokens of the Divine Presence among them, the Israelites prepare for the capture of Jericho. But, in this, as in the crossing of the Jordan, every human device is superseded, and wondrously simple and strangely novel methods are prescribed. Amidst them all, however, " the ark of the covenant " is the grand instrument for effecting everything. Hence, let us contemplate

II. *The solemn procession of the ark round the walls of Jericho.*

1. For six days, the ark was to be carried, still by priests, around the whole circuit of the city. It was to be preceded by seven other priests, each with a simple ram's-horn trumpet, which they blew as they went. Before them marched a band of veteran warriors, more to clear the way than to guard it : and, then, behind the ark followed the main body of the people. Whether they were to march at the same reverent distance from it, as when they were advancing to the banks of the river, we are not told. While marching thither, they were not to come nearer to the ark than about half a mile, apparently that every individual in a long line of march, might see for himself that which was to be their guide and regulator. (Josh. III. 4.) Be this as it may, one special injunction was laid upon them which had not been laid before. They were to observe the utmost silence. (Joshua VI. 10.)

" And Joshua had commanded the people, saying, Ye shall not shout nor make any noise with your voice, neither shall any word proceed out of your mouth, until the day I bid you shout : then shall ye shout."

2. So singular an arrangement as this must have arrested

the attention of the king and warriors of Jericho. They
had, as Rahab had previously told the spies, heard of the
passage of the Red Sea, and were faint with fear at what
they heard. Now, also, the terror of the Lord was upon
the city, and though, from what is elsewhere incidentally
said, (Joshua xxiv. 11.) it is probable that they shot their
missiles from their walls, yet none had the daring to sally
out and attack the Hebrews.

For a whole army to march, day after day, round the
city, with no other sound but a few rustic trumpets, was a
military procedure which no General in Canaan had ever
heard. But, it is probable that, as those trumpets were
blown by the priests of Jehovah, their sound was divinely
impulsive, and tremendously thrilling to every ear in Jericho.
It is more than probable, too, that the sight of the ark was
attended with strange sensations to the men of Jericho, beyond anything of which the men of Israel themselves were
sensible. For, as in the passage of the Red Sea, the Lord
looked from out of the pillar of cloud and troubled the
Egyptians, so may it have been that, from the radiance of
the ark, He glanced at the men of Jericho in a manner
which conveyed mysterious terror to them. They felt an
unspeakable awe, and a dismal foreboding, which, yet,
perhaps, no man dared acknowledge to his fellow. The
continuance of this silent spectacle might embolden some
few monster hearts, and incline them to banter and jest;
but it is probable that the majority of them suspected and
dreaded something answerable to their own enchantments,
or demon-arts of magic. At all events, the six days march
must have left them with strange and mingled imaginings,
in which their own oracles could give them no aid.

3. But now, on the seventh day, which the Jews generally believe to have been a Sabbath-day, a laborious march is followed by an easy and most triumphant victory. If the day were the Sabbath, we are sure that the Lord of it consecrated it to the special service of the capture of a wicked city, which, though a strange work, was nevertheless the Lord's own work. One at least of the seven days must have been a Sabbath-day. If that day fell on one of the six, then was the march round the city, little more perhaps, than the legitimate "Sabbath-day's journey." Still, in either case, as there was a marshalling of troops, and other secular doings, the pious Hebrew exercised faith in the Lord of the Sabbath, and believed that He had power to vary his own law respecting the sanctity of the Sabbath. The sect of the Pharisees had not yet risen up to trouble honest minds with petty quibbles.

On that day, all the people "rose up early about the dawning of the day," and began a seven-times march round the city. At the end of the seventh circuit, the priests sounded with additional energy, and all the people, at the bidding of Joshua, raised "a very great shout." In that moment, the entire wall of the city, said, by the Jews, to be of seven-fold width, "*fell down flat.*" An unseen hand dashed it all to the ground, instantly, entirely, levelly. Which last circumstance, namely, that it fell down *flat*, or levelly, was not the least remarkable of any, because nothing but a special power of divine exertion could have effected such a phenomenon. Lofty and massy walls, when overthrown by any ordinary means, fall confusedly, and in rugged heaps. But the walls of this God-captured city fall down *flatly*, as though on purpose to facilitate the entrance of the Hebrews into it; for it is significantly added, "So that the people went up into the city, every man *straight before him*, and they took the city." Then followed the work of righteous extermination: righteous, we say, because, sanguinary as it may seem to us, it was executed at the bidding of a holy God.

4. So marvellous a capture, however, was not merely an exertion of divine power, exercised without any reference to human intervention: it was visibly divine, but co-operatively human. Though no skill or strength of man was employed in the overthrow of the walls, yet was the faith of the Lord's people largely expressed. In the army of Israel was a goodly band of spiritual soldiers, who believed and prayed while they gazed or shouted: for St. Paul certifies us that "*By faith* the walls of Jericho fell down, after they were compassed about seven days."

An overthrow so sudden and signal is left on record, also, to furnish us with some idea of those manifestations of Almighty power which will, doubtless, be exhibited in the day of the destruction of Anti-Christ, when it shall be said, "Babylon is fallen, is fallen!" The fall will be as sudden, as awful, as effectual as that of Jericho. Sinners will be as secure in the fastnesses of their superstition, as the men of Jericho were in their apparently impregnable walls. But, their judgment will be as certain, and, probably, as instantaneous.

III. *The defeat of Israel at Ai, and the consequent falling down of Joshua before "the ark of the covenant,"* were consequent upon a forbidden act in the capture of Jericho.

The people were commanded, in that capture, to abstain from appropriating a single article of value to themselves. All the gold and silver was to be consecrated to the Lord. Spite, however, of this solemn command, one Achan secreted a wedge of gold. The curse of the theft pervaded the whole camp. It spread as a blight over every effort of the people. The consequence was that, when they went out to attack the next city, they were grievously repulsed. Upon a recurrence of this humiliating disaster, Joshua and all the elders of Israel prostrated themselves before the ark of the Lord*—Joshua VII. 6. This falling down of Joshua and the elders was for prayerful inquiry of the God of the ark, and not for any superstitious reverence of the ark itself. Jehovah acknowledged the act, and honoured it by an explanatory response. The criminal was detected. The crime was expiated; and Israel was righted. The whole circumstance was calculated to teach all men the evil of covetousness, the omniscience and holiness of Jehovah, and the certainty with which He will detect and punish sin. It, also, very affectingly admonishes us of our liability to suffer the effects of the divine displeasure, through the guilt of intimate connections, on the principle that, if one member becomes gangrenous, the adjoining members are likely to languish.

But, harmless and holy as was the act of Joshua in falling down before the ark, Antichrist steps in and turns it into a plea for superstition and idolatry. Like certain venomous

* "And Joshua rent his clothes, and fell to the earth upon his face, before the ark of the Lord, until the eventide, he and the elders of Israel, and put dust upon their heads."

creatures, which first inject poison, and then suck it out, the Papal Antichrist first infuses falsehood into parts of the sacred history, and then parades it for the sanction of blasphemous doctrine.

The case is this: Because there were on the mercy-seat of the ark figures of cherubim, and Joshua in falling down before the ark necessarily fell down before *them*, therefore, say Roman Catholic Doctors, we are justified in doing the like before images of Christ, his mother, and other saints, as well as altars of the host. The plea is formally stated in the note of the Rhemish version of the New Testament, on the word " cherubim," in the fifth verse of the ninth chapter of the Epistle to the Hebrews. The plea is as disingenuous as it is wicked; because it keeps out of sight the true facts of the case, as well as foists in ideas which have no manner of relation to it.

Joshua fell down before the ark, not because of the cherubim upon it, but because of the Shekinah which rested between them, as the visible symbol of the invisible God. He, therefore, prostrated himself before the ark not as an *image* of God, but as the seat of God Himself. God was actually there on the ark, and not merely represented by it. But, *is Christ actually in any of the images of Him* which deluded votaries first fabricate and then worship? The question hardly needs an answer. Moreover, when Joshua fell down before the ark, it is more than probable that he neither *saw* the ark nor the cherubim on it. It was covered by a curtain, if not by the tent which was made on purpose to cover it. Here, again, is no resemblance between the act of Joshua and the prostrations of those who gaze intently on the glaring or gaudy figures of Christ and the Virgin Mary.

We must, further, take into our account the immense difference between God's positive command for the building of the ark as one single vessel, for the holding of the law, to be concealed from the people, and the unbidden, or rather the forbidden, formation not of vessels but of images of persons, and those images almost numberless in their amount. Altogether, the perversion of the entire case is as odious, and as sickening, as we fear the crime of it is monstrous and damnable. May God in mercy and pity spare and turn all those who are deceived by the deceiver, lest they be destroyed by the Destroyer.

IV. *The muster of the tribes in two divisions, on Mount Ebal and Mount Gerizim*, when the ark, as our text states, was set between them, was the last of the four instances, in which, during the government of Joshua, that ark is mentioned.

As the narrative stands in our Bible, the time of that muster of the tribes was shortly after the conquest of Ai, which had given the people so much trouble. But some commentators are disposed to think that the passage is transposed, and that it ought to be referred to a later period of the history. There is, however, no need for any chronological alteration. At all events, the narrative itself is fraught with solemn and elevating interest. It is briefly of this nature: Moses had strictly enjoined the elders and the people that, upon their establishment in Canaan, they should assemble at a definite spot, which he distinctly described, though he had never seen it. The spot was in

Shechem, where two small mountains, or pointed hills, were so near together, that a voice from the intervening valley could be easily heard on either. In this valley the noble and faithful Joshua caused the ark to be brought, and took his station near it. To the people who were posted on the two hills, and in the presence of all the chiefs and worthies of the nation, he audibly recited the curses and the blessings to which Jehovah had bidden the whole multitude to add their solemn and earnest "Amen." It was, in fact, a sort of "Commination Service," as our church uses the phrase; and yet it was accompanied with many circumstances of affecting grandeur. Never did the ark of the covenant cast its golden splendours on a scene more transcendantly beautiful. The locality, as travellers report, must have been lovely. Stationed on two such contiguous hills all Israel were seen at once, and saw each other. Veterans and younger warriors, mothers and children, with many a varied individual, were grouped according to their tribes. In the valley gleamed the ark, aud stood the princes of the people. Many a heart throbbed with recollections of the wonder-paved way in which God had led them: and many an eye paid its crystal tribute to the gratitude which demanded it. And, then, what more in keeping with the entire scene could there be than the heavenly aspect of the man who was the type of the God-man—Jesus—the true Joshua and Saviour of the Church? There stood he, the Lord's own chosen one, reciting from the standard copy of the Book of the Law, all that Moses had divinely enjoined. But, we must not trace out the solemnly glorious scene any further. May the God of the ark send upon us much of the Spirit which actuated Joshua and all the sound-hearted ones around him.

Suffice it to add that, after this occurrence, no further mention is expressly made of the ark during the life of Joshua. In the eighteenth chapter of this Book, and in the first verse, we are informed that the tabernacle was, at length, set up in Shiloh, and the ark was, of course, deposited in the western end of it—under the tent which was made for it. Shiloh was a central spot, in the lot of the tribe to which Joshua belonged, and which, probably, was the home of his old age. Here the ark continued for nearly three hundred years; during various vicissitudes of Israel's history, to the leading incidents of which, as connected with the ark, your attention will be invited (D.V.) in the next lecture.

In closing the present lecture, it cannot be inapplicable to point out to you

1. *The serial sort of connexion* which seems to exist between these four events which we have been considering. The former two were marked by miracle, the other two by devotion. Of the miraculous incidents, one was miracle rising superior to the regularities of nature, the other was miracle leaping the barriers of human art. Divine power rolled back the stream of Jordan, and the same almighty force threw down in scorn the human-builded walls of Jericho. Of the devotional acts, one was the offering of supplication, and the other the reading of the Word of God. Both these are highly admonitory, and all are particularly instructive. Miracles may dazzle us; but everything devotional should

engage and interest us. We should be ready, not only with the Psalmist to look back upon the wondrous scene and exclaim, " What ailed thee—thou Jordan, that thou wast driven back?" (Ps. cxiv. 5.) but we should, also, delight to say, "I will lift up my hands towards thy holy oracle." "Oh how I love thy law, it is my meditation all the day."

2 *The greater wonders which await the eyes of all the followers of the true Joshua.* What the Lord Jesus said to Nathaniel respecting, most likely, the vision of Jacob's ladder, may be fitly applied to us, when rising from the contemplation of what Jehovah wrought in the Jordan and at Jericho, namely, "Thou shalt see greater things than these." God's wonders of old are but pattern shadows of the astonishing realities which his Church is destined to witness. His arm has yet to be made bare in the sight, not of one or two nations only, but of all people. The followers of the Lamb shall walk through a deeper river than the Jordan, and enjoy the protection of a brighter Ark than that which stayed its impetuous flood. They shall, too, behold "the pulling down of strongholds" by an invisible arm, even the fortresses and high towers of Satan's erection, in the Jerichos which for ages he has held and garrisoned. Meanwhile, may miracles of grace be wrought in our hearts, and the True Ark dwell in them!

3. *The necessity of keeping our eye on that True Ark, and the suitableness of a residence brought nearer and still nearer to it, as age advances.* Israel so followed the Ark under the guidance of Joshua, as not only to hear of it, but to see it. The eye of our faith is to be constantly kept upon Christ.

And, if we come to be settled in some quiet Shiloh, for a calm old age, let us make it our greatest solace to have that Ark very nigh unto us, so nigh that even when we tread the verge of Jordan, all anxious fears may subside, and our faith rest calmly upon the same sure Ark of our salvation, Jesus Christ the Righteous.

LECTURE IV.

"And when the people were come into the camp, the elders of Israel said, Wherefore hath the Lord smitten us to day before the Philistines? Let us fetch the ark of the covenant of the Lord out of Shiloh unto us, that, when it cometh among us, it may save us out of the hand of our enemies.

"So the people went to Shiloh, that they might bring from thence the ark of the covenant of the Lord of hosts, which dwelleth between the cherubims: and the two sons of Eli, Hophni and Phineas, were there with the ark of the covenant of God."—1 Samuel, iv. 3, 4.

IT was proposed that the subject of the present lecture should be " The History of the Ark of the Covenant under the Judges." By "the Judges" we are to understand those governors of Israel who followed each other, at broken intervals, from the death of Joshua to the reign of Saul. The times of the Judges stretched over an historic period of more than three centuries. That period was like the gradual approach of an eclipse. The death of Joshua and of the Elders who were his companions, was the signal of its commencement. After them, the sun of Israel soon became dim. Notwithstanding occasional gleams of light, darkness began to prevail. Jehovah was slighted, and the local gods of the land were cherished. Chastisements and deliverances followed each other like the alternations of gloom and gleam, from flitting clouds, on the day of an eclipse. At length, during the high priesthood of Eli, when his lewd sons, Hophni and Phineas, hastened on the iniquity of the land, the total obscuration of Israel's sun set in, Philistine darkness swallowed up the light of the ark, and the glory of Israel fell beneath the dank cloud of Dagon.

It is painfully remarkable that, all through the Book of Judges, no mention is made of the ark till the last chapter but one. In that chapter (xx. 27.) it is parenthetically said, that "the ark of the covenant of God was there (i.e. in Shiloh) in those days." Joshua had set up the tabernacle there, and deposited the ark in it. Thither, with more or less punctuality, the people, after his time, continued to go up, according to the law. But, as was predicted of them, they soon began to fall away into foolish and hurtful idolatries. According to prevailing custom, they adopted the gods of the native inhabitants of the land: for, long before and long after their settlement in Canaan, they were infected with the heathen notion that certain deities presided over certain districts. On going, therefore, into a new locality, they were tempted to follow the gods of it. Not that they always or altogether discarded the worship of Jehovah, but added to it the worship of idols. This was the sin of Israel in even the after days of Isaiah and Jeremiah, just as it is the sin of all nominal Christians up to the present hour, who have not the honesty to reject Christ, but aim to unite the profession of his name with the love of the world or some favourite Baal.

Things in Israel proceeded from bad to worse, till Eli became the aged high priest at Shiloh. He was a good man at heart, but sadly irresolute in mind. His sons made themselves detestably vile, but he restrained them not. At length, their conduct, as priests, was so profligate and atrocious, that God issued a sentence of extermination against them and the entire family.

Our text brings us to the period, when, in connexion with the eclipse of the ark, themselves were about to be consigned to utter darkness. But, lo! just as that eclipse and that darkness begin, God raises up a star in the distant horizon, which is to pour its light upon Israel, and to be the harbinger of a brighter day. Samuel is born, in answer to Eli's prediction, and soon he ministers to the Lord, and sleeps near the ark in Shiloh. There the Lord, one eventful night, called him by name, and spoke to him solemn words. It was after midnight, and towards the approach of morning, when the lamps in the tabernacle were burning dimly, and flickering in their last drops of oil. Apt time this to represent the waning state of Eli's priesthood, and Israel's prosperity, as well as the opening dawn of Samuel's prophetic rule.

But, as indicative of that infatuation which precedes destruction, the Israelites, apparently without consulting Samuel, determine to rally a war against the Philistines. They accordingly muster their forces and join in battle. They fight, but conquer not. Four thousand of them are slain, and they fall back to consult with themselves only what to do. They fretfully ask, "Wherefore hath the Lord smitten us to day before the Philistines?" Had they consulted Him at His ark in Shiloh, they would soon have learned why He had smitten them. But, as conscience whispered *why*, they stifled that monitor, and set up their own mad will for their guide. "Let us, (said they) fetch the ark of the covenant of the Lord out of Shiloh unto us, that when it cometh among us, it may save us out of the hand of our enemies."

In the history which follows this insane and wicked proposal, we have to contemplate the desecration and loss of the ark, the vengeance which followed its capture, and the admonitory account of its recovery. May we find abundant profit in reaping the rich instruction with which this history is charged.

I. *The desecration and loss of the ark* formed a melancholy feature in Israel's portraiture.

1. To send for the ark from its quiet resting place, and to force it into the din of a field of battle, was not only an unwarrantable, but a most wicked procedure. The evident intention of those who sent for it was to put themselves under the protection of it as a charm or "*fetish.*" That "*it* (said they) may *save* us." Eli, most likely, had no voice allowed him in the matter; and his profligate sons were but too ready to comply with a profane project. They were as willing as the people, whom they had served to corrupt and debase—to venerate the ark merely as a visible symbol: for wicked priests are generally the most zealous in outside formalities. Accordingly, Hophni and Phineas accompany the ark to the field of battle. They went, most

likely, not as its bearers, but as its lordly superintendents. When the ark arrived in the camp, " all Israel shouted with a great shout, so that the earth rang again." The shout reached the ears of the Philistines, and gave them a temporary chill ; but it did not do with them as when Israel shouted before the walls of Jericho. The God of Joshua was in the shout then, because He was with the ark. But He was now absent from both. The people had sent for the ark, not for Him. They, therefore, had " their heart's desire, but leanness withal."

2. And now the Hebrews renew the battle, and carry the ark into the midst of the fray ; just as the ancient heathen used to carry the images of their gods among their fighting men ; and as, in some sort, modern Roman Catholics do on the continent, with the canopy of the host, or the images of the Virgin Mary and the Infant Jesus, when a city is besieged, or a neighbourhood is visited with pestilence. The carrying, in fact, of the Bambino, as it is called, from the church to which it belongs to the houses of the sick who can pay for its visit, in the city of Rome itself, is but a wretched mimickry of this carrying of the ark for the securing of victory.

The result, in regard to the people of Israel, was what might easily have been foreseen. Fighting under a false confidence, they sustained a terrible defeat. Their loss, as if to mark their presumption in fetching the ark, was far greater than before. Instead of losing four thousand men, they lost " thirty thousand footmen." Dreadful lesson this to all who depend on a false peace, while, by their continuance in sin, they court a fearful destruction ! Besides this loss of men, God suffers his ark to be taken. The Philistines seize it, and bear it off in triumph. Was Jehovah forgetful, or—dare we say it?—unwise, in allowing this? He condescended to show that He was neither. He was preparing a scourge for his enemies, a rebuke for his people, and lessons for them and us. Philistia was to loathe the ark; Israel to long for it; and all Christendom to learn from it. Yes, we are to learn (and the lesson is becoming every day more and more necessary) that God's choicest ordinances are nothing to Him, when his professed worshippers trust in them, and not in Himself. If men trust in sacraments, or any outward symbol, and crave them, send for them, and use them, as Israel, under the countenance of Hophni and Phineas, sent for and used the ark, God will abandon them as He abandoned the ark, and leave his formal and faithless worshippers either to die in their sin, or fall into the hand of their enemy. No greater or surer curse can befal our own beloved church than the prevalence of zeal for the ark without any corresponding zeal for the God of the ark; an increase of reverence for the forms and rituals of Christianity, without a proportionate increase of love for the doctrine and person of Christ. The good Lord save us from such a calamity!

3. Connected with the capture of the ark was the death of kindred, in three very different and yet very painful instances.

(1.) Hophni and Phineas were slain together, apparently close to the ark, and, most likely, in fighting for its defence. They went out with it to the field of fight, like sheep doomed for slaughter. God had said that they should both be slain in one day. They, perhaps, had heard the threat, and despised it. Least of all did they imagine that they *could* die while holding to the ark. But, they did die; and in their death we read this appalling truth, namely, that men may battle unto death for the externals of true religion, and yet be neither believers nor martyrs. Many have stood in the temple, and held to the ark, and cried "Lord, Lord!" without being acknowledged as good and faithful servants. We must judge of faith, confessorship, and martyrdom, by other rules than those of mere external attachments.

(2.) On hearing the news, not of the defeat of Israel, but of the capture of the ark, the aged Eli fell down and brake his neck. He heard of the ark's departure to the camp, and his heart trembled for its safety. A secret boding came upon him. He followed it as far as he was able, to the gate of the city. He there sat down with a boding, an almost breaking heart. The first mention of the taking of the ark increased Eli's anguish beyond endurance; and then followed the heavy backward fall and consequent fracture of the old man's neck. With solemnity, then, and sadness we gaze upon the fact that a really good man may end his days under chastisement and the deepest gloom. A father, too, may die with the love of God in his heart, while his sons perish in their hatred of that God. Awful but salutary lessons for christians, whether children or parents!

(3.) In addition to Hophni, Phineas, and Eli, dies the gentle wife of one of the two wicked sons. Phineas, though a lewd and profligate man, had a chaste and pious wife. She, perhaps, loved him, and doubtless prayed for him. It was her duty to do both. Possibly, she deprecated his going with the ark : and, like her father-in-law, had many a melancholy misgiving respecting it. It was, also, so ordered that the time for the birth of her babe was drawing nigh. The news of the loss of the ark accelerated that time. She became a mother, but heeded not the joy of a man-child being born into the world. The ark of her God was gone, and nothing worth living for remained. She revived and spoke only just so far as to discover her piety and her grief. "She named the child Ichabod," which, in our marginal bibles, is translated "There is no glory ;" or "Where is the glory ?" In the ensuing verse it is added, "And she said, the glory is departed from Israel, *for the ark of God is taken.*"

4. And, now, the Philistines, having seized the ark as their most splendid trophy, convey it to Ashdod, one of their five cities, because the temple of their god Dagon was there. In that temple, and by the hideous image of that no-god, they placed "the ark of the covenant" of the living God. O, piteous spectacle! O, melancholy sight! O, most grievous indignity! How could Moses have endured it? or Joshua, how would he have borne the thought of it? The holy ark set by the side of a filthy idol, and as a trophy, too, in the gorgeous temple of that idol! Did not the hearts of Israel burn to risk their blood in the forcible rescue of it. Did the heavens show no sign of displeasure at such a scene? Was there no falling star, no bursting cloud, no lightning-bolt, to beat down the temple, and set the ark of God free? Alas, for Israel! They had lost their father's piety, and so had lost their father's valor. Jehovah shewed, as yet, no sign. He had other purposes to fulfil.

Let us proceed to contemplate

II. *The vengeance which followed the capture of the ark by the Philistines.*

What they really intended by carrying it to the temple and presence of Dagon is not quite clear. They may have meant to express their belief in Dagon's power as having brought them the prize : or to show honour to their god as alone worthy of such a prize : or to make use of it on some festal day for their sport, as they had done with Samson : or to garnish some triumphal procession when offering sacrifice to Dagon ; or, as some conjecture, to worship it in conjunction with Dagon, according to the very common practice of heathen nations. Be these things as they may, the people and priests of Ashdod had only one brief night of quiet, one short dream of triumph, as masters of the ark. They were even eager for that night to be gone, and that dream to brighten into more intense reality ; for, it is said, " They of Ashdod arose *early* on the morrow." But now their disasters begin. Like a multitude of dwarfs, making sport around one of their own giants, when slumbering after toil, the Philistines find to their cost that they were sporting with, or glorying in the possession of the ark of God's strength, which, by gradual efforts, soon taught them a strange lesson.

1. On entering their temple early on the first morning, they find their idol prostrate on the ground. In the course of the night, unseen hands had thrown down Dagon flat " upon his face to the earth." The fall was very significant too, for Dagon lay, where themselves ought to have bowed as penitent worshippers, right "before the ark of the Lord."

Their annoyance and alarm must have been great. Nevertheless, they do their best to suppress all emotion, and hasten to " set Dagon in his place again." No doubt they make his standing as fast as possible, and frame clever excuses for the catastrophe.

2. But, their work and their wit are fruitless. Another night ensues, and again, in the early morn, they resort to the temple, only, however, to witness a far more surprising and vexatious spectacle. It is thus described (1 Sam. v. 4.)

"And when they arose early on the morrow morning, behold Dagon was fallen upon his face to the ground before the ark of the Lord; and the head of Dagon and both the palms of his hands were cut off upon the threshold; only the stump of Dagon was left to him."

" The stump of Dagon " was the lower or fish-like half of the monster idol; for all historians agree in describing the figure of Dagon as resembling that of the fabled *merman*. The breaking off of the head and the hands was a token to the Philistines that their god had neither wisdom nor might; for the head was the emblem of the one, and the hands of the other.

3, Striking, however, and undeniable as this prodigy was, did it startle the Philistine priests, or turn them from their superstition? By no means; but rather, as is usual in all similar cases, hardened and confirmed them in it. Instead of learning a single lesson from the sharp fact of their idol's head and hands being deliberately placed in the most humiliating part of the temple, on the threshold, where, also, they were compelled to see the severed pieces, they actually convert the incident into a fresh incentive of superstitious reverence. They made it a plea for sanctimoniously

stepping over the threshold instead of stepping upon it.
This is a striking and an instructive fact for us to ponder in
the present day. But, I cannot preferably teach you its
general import than by quoting to you a remark of Bishop
Hall. "It is just with God that those who want grace shall
"want wit too. *It is the power of superstition to turn men
"into those stocks and stones which they worship.* "They that
"make them are like unto them." Never was the genius
of superstition more accurately defined than by this masterly
exposition of the Psalmist's words. Alas, for its too truthful application to the giant superstition of Christendom!
Popery has a mysterious power of turning its votaries into
itself. And what is itself? Let Holy Scripture supply the
answer. It is a system of ecclesiastical "sorcery," a circle
of "seducing spirits," an army of mouths "speaking lies
in hypocrisy," an engine which works "with all deceivable-
ness of unrighteousness." In a word, it is an imposture as
great as that of Dagon; and it comprises as many absurdi-
ties and as much sottishness as that comprised.* They who
embrace it gradually become like it: except where the
Spirit of God has more influence on the heart than in the
head. Upon no other ground can we account for that painfully strange phenomenon which has of late been so frequently forced upon our observation, namely, the fact that,
when English clergymen join the Church of Rome, they
seem to lose not merely their common sense, but their

* The flight of the Pope from Rome in 1848, (so ominously
anticipated by Fleming) instead of being a check to Romanism, was
made by its partizans a call for sympathy and greater devotedness.
Even the destruction of Rome itself will effect no conversion. See
Rev. xviii. 9.

truthfulness, and that disposition to adhere to fair, open, honorable dealing, which marks and almost makes the character of the English gentleman.

4. After the demolition of Dagon in his own temple, without any sign of change in priests or people, Jehovah began to scourge them strangely and severely.

"But the hand of the Lord was heavy upon them of Ashdod, and he destroyed them, and smote them with emerods, even Ashdod and the coasts thereof.—1 Samuel v. 6.

This infliction of death and dreadful disease, probably as novel to the Philistines as it was excruciating and annoying, had the effect of urging the men of Ashdod to discern the cause of their visitation, and to take measures for the removal of the ark. The lords of the Philistines determined on its transport to Gath, as though, forsooth, the ark might fancy another city more than Ashdod. To Gath it went, but the same deadly and disastrous consequences followed it. The giants of that city, as well as its dwarfs, fell under the blows of the same mysterious power; for "The Lord smote the men of the city, both small and great." "Therefore, (it is added) they sent the ark of the Lord to Ekron;" where the same terrible inflictions visited them, "for there was a deadly destruction throughout all the city." The consequence was that the Ekronites, as is generally inferred, carried the ark out of their city into the open fields. But, there, again, judgment began to work in a new and a startling manner. Enormous multitudes of mice sprang up, spread about, and consumed the produce of the land. Thus, that little elegant creature the field mouse, was employed as God's advocate and executioner. It taught the Philistine farmers WHO was "the Lord of the whole earth," and punished them for not believing in Him.

5. At last, in right earnest, people, priests, and lords, all resolutely set about ridding themselves of so fearful a deity as the ark. Like the Gadarenes of later days, they wish it to depart out of their coasts; and like as with those people, too, the wish was the result of infidel fear, and unrelenting attachment to their own superstitions.

The Philistine project was to send away the ark in a new cart drawn by two suckling kine, accompanied by costly offerings, golden mice, and golden representations of their disease, and to let those kine go whither they pleased; if into the land of Israel all the better, as they would then be sure of the ark being in its proper country. Hence we have now to consider

III. *The admonitory account of the restoration of the ark.*

The Philistine device of untrained kine drawing a new cart at random was a presumption on their part, but an over-ruling providence on the part of Jehovah. He permitted it for the manifestation of his glorious power. The kine, though never yoked before, and while actually lowing after their calves, nevertheless turn away from them, and take the straight road to Bethshemesh, a town of Israel. —1 Samuel vi. 12. The entire circumstance was a divine prodigy. It showed not only the creator's power in restraining the natural instinct of the kine in leaving their calves, but his invisible presence in guiding them along the right road to a town of Israel.

1. And, now, after seven month's absence from that

land, the ark returns thereto by the miraculous intervention of that God who had first permitted its capture and removal therefrom.

The kine drew the cart into the field of one Joshua, a Bethshemite. The people in it were reaping, and they "rejoiced," it is said, at seeing the ark. Alas, for their joy, because it had no true-heartedness in it! They had no joy in the God of the ark, and had learned nothing from its absence. In the effervescence of their carnal delight, they slew the kine on the spot, and though a very irregular proceeding, as males only were to be so offered, they burned them in sacrifice with the wood of the cart which they had drawn.*

Bethshemesh, it should be remembered, was a city of priests. Levites, therefore, came and first took the ark out of the cart, and set it upon a great stone which was in the field, and which afterwards was called the "The great stone of Abel," i.e., of "*weeping*," because of the after weeping of the people of the city.

From either vain curiosity or over officiousness, the men of Bethshemesh looked into the ark, and thus incurred the divine displeasure. They might have pretended that they looked in order to see if the Philistines had molested or marred the tables of the law. But it was not their business or vocation to make such an inquest. We are never warranted to do that which under no circumstances ought to be done. God is the arbiter and responsible dispenser of

---

* Possibly they thought that animals which had been miraculously acted upon, and used for so divine a purpose, ought not to return to common uses in a pagan land.

all such cases. The issue to the Bethshemites was "a great slaughter," either by pestilence or sudden death. It is, too, probable, that they were, as a priestly community, an indolent and godless population, for we read not of any pains on their part to lodge the ark, or pay to it such becoming attention as others were eager to render.

2, The Bethshemites, evidently in an impenitent and querulous temper, send to the inhabitants of Kirjath-jearim, a town of Judah, to fetch away the ark. They showed their unworthiness of being the guardians of such a treasure, for, instead of humbling themselves, they sought to be rid of a high and hallowed responsibility. The men, however, of Kirjath-jearim were far more noble than they; though it does not appear that they had a single priest among them. They promptly fetched the ark to their town, and lodged it in what we should call the high house of the place; for "they brought it into the house of Abinadab in the hill." This person was probably a Levite, and is said by the Jews to have been a very honourable and very holy man. If so, we may be sure that his honour was increased, and his holiness turned into his greater happiness, by having in his house the ark of the infinitely holy God.

His son—perhaps his only son—was consecrated, or specially set apart, "to keep the ark of the Lord," that is, to keep the apartment in proper order in which it was lodged, and to do everything which reverence and piety dictated to be done. All which bespeaks a high degree of religious propriety on the part of Abinadab, and greatly contrasts with the apathy of the Israelites generally. The consecration of his son was an ecclesiastical irregularity: but the affairs of the nation were so grievously distracted, that little else could be expected. In times of national confusion, the church generally suffers disorder. Sound and faithful men must then do the best they can.

The tarriance of the ark at Kirjath-jearim was long and lamentable. It could not have been for less than forty years; for the twenty years mentioned in 1 Sam. VII. 2, referred to the period which elapsed from the removal of the ark to Kirjath-jearim, to the date of the narrative which immediately follows the mention of those years. Towards the end of those years, the people, under the stirring ministry and bright example of Samuel, began to consider their ways, and to exercise godly sorrow for the error of them. It is consequently said, "All the house of Israel lamented after the Lord."

Still, for wise reasons, God did not stir up any one to carry back the ark to Shiloh, or to bring the tabernacle to it. The priests and people of Shiloh had participated too deeply in the sins of Hophni and Phineas, for the Holy God ever again to trust his ark among them. "He forsook the tabernacle at Shiloh." Because He valued true piety more than gaudy formality, He chose to leave the ark in the house of a mere Levite or private individual, rather than to consign it to the charge of even authorized priests; just as he has, many times since, sent His Gospel into a cave or a cabin, when the ministers of a costly edifice have corrupted or cared but little for it.

Suffer me, in concluding this Lecture, to point out to you a few topics for your earnest consideration.

1. *All that we have hitherto been contemplating*, in the

F

history of the ark of the covenant, *is plaintively but most poetically summed up*, by Asaph the psalmist, in Psalm LXXVIII, 54—68. This is one proof that God wishes the history of his Church to be remembered, and intends his people to cheer and strengthen themselves by the contemplation of his mighty acts and his wonders of old.

2. *It is dangerous as well as foolish to slight or abuse our spiritual privileges.* The presence of the ark was a high distinction and a noble privilege for the large town of Shiloh. Many temporal, as well as many spiritual, interests were involved in its location. But, Shiloh eventually lost them all, because it lost the ark. For a time, indeed, the tabernacle continued to stand there, but its life and glory were gone. The sun had left the firmament, and a dark and deathly night followed. The materials of the tabernacle began, as the Jews say, to decay and rot, after the ark was taken from it, whereas, while the ark was in it, the whole textile fabric, like their apparel in the wilderness, suffered nothing from weather or wear.

Oh that all who hear these things would lay to heart the admonition they convey! If we lose the presence of Christ in our parish, our church, or our home, we lose all that is valuable in life for ourselves and our children. If once we tempt Him to withdraw it from us, He may never allow it to return, just as the ark never came back to Shiloh. "Spare us, Good Lord!"

3. *The vicissitudes of the true Church are not intended to discourage, but to admonish us.* They always carry with them the elements of hope. Out of their darker phases, God has been bringing light, while his people have mourned the

while for the want of light. Samuel was in fair training to become a living representation of Jehovah, while Eli was waning, and the ark was trembling on the shoulders of its godless bearers. While the ark, too, was unloved in the land of the Philistines, many a heart was secretly moved to desire it among the thousands of Israel. And while, also, it was lodging in a private dwelling at Kirjath-jearim, that child was born of Jesse, at Bethlehem, who was to prepare a new tabernacle for it in Zion, and to give the plan of a temple for it in Jerusalem. The lodging of the ark in the house of Abinadab, within the precincts of Judah, was, in fact, a quiet step towards its ultimate destination. It was the bringing of it into the lot of that very tribe from which the True Ark was to originate. It was, also, the placing of it in a spot favourable for its transit to Jerusalem. And, yet, at the time, no eye, perhaps, foresaw this ; nor did any heart thrill with delight in anticipation of the noble songs which David, by the Spirit, would compose for being sung before it. So true is it that " light is sown for the righteous," during the hours of their darkness : and gladness of heart is being prepared for them, when they are most sorrowful.

LECTURE V.

"Now therefore arise, O Lord God, into thy resting place, Thou, and the ark of thy strength : let thy priests, O Lord God be clothed with salvation, and let thy saints rejoice in goodness."—2 Chronicles vi. 41.

THESE words form the conclusion of Solomon's magnificent address, when he had brought " the ark of the covenant" to its final resting place,—i.e., within the holy of holies of his newly-erected temple. The words, also, occur in Psalm cxxxii. 8, where they appear in a curtailed form. Both the longer and the shorter form, however, are said to be Solomon's; for the composition of that Psalm is generally attributed to him. But, as that Psalm contains especial reference to David, as desiring to lodge the ark in a place somewhat worthy of it, we hereby obtain a clue to that series of events which affected the ark, during the reigns of David and Solomon. Those events may be comprised under the following divisions :—first, the commencement of David's preparations for the removal of the ark from its obscurity, and the check which he received in them ; second, the renewal of his preparations, and the success which attended them; and, third, the elevation of the ark by Solomon to its grand and final resting place. May our meditation on these topics be sweet and profitable.

It should first be mentioned, by way of reminder, that we have traced the ark from the time of its construction under Moses all through its marvellous progress under Joshua, till he lodged it at Shiloh, and during its tarriance there under the Judges till its capture by the Philistines and its restoration to Israel. In our last lecture we left it at Kirjath-jearim, otherwise called Baale or Baalah, a town of Judah—at no great distance to the west of Jerusalem. Here it was lodged—in the house of Abinadab—who was a Levite, as some think, or only a private but true Israelite, as others say. Here, also, it remained, in comparative obscurity, during the greater part of Samuel's rule, and all through the reign of Saul. That self-willed monarch was too indifferent with regard to divine things to take thought for "the ark of the covenant." It is mentioned only once during the period of his reign—1 Samuel XIV. 18, in which case it seems that he desired the presence of the ark, now that Samuel had left him, to serve him for divination in difficulties and perplexities. When, however, David succeeded Saul, and found himself well established in the kingdom, he formed the pious design of bringing the ark from its obscurity to his own metropolis. As the man after God's own heart, he dearly loved the things of God, and made the honour and furtherance of them the first business of his life: just as all the genuine people of God delight and glory in the advancement of the cause of God.

I. *The commencement of David's preparations for the removal of the ark, and the painful check which he sustained in them,* are somewhat thus :

1. He consulted with all the leaders of Israel—civil, military, and ecclesiastical—about bringing the ark to Jerusalem. With wondrous unanimity they concurred in his wishes, and most zealously devoted themselves to the carrying of them out. But, as nothing is definitely said of David's *consulting* God in the matter, nor of his taking pains for everything connected with it to be done with due order, we cannot be surprised when we find that the course was not so smooth and favourable as might be expected. We are hereby admonished that, although, in our undertakings, we proceed after extensive deliberation, we are on a very insecure footing, if we have failed in taking counsel with God. Failure in that point may prove a flaw in our writ of success which may subject us to the sharpest disappointment.

2. On a set day, David proceeded with a multitudinous gathering of soldiers and people to the town of Kirjath-jearim. The account is recorded in 2 Samuel vi., and in 1 Chronicles xiii., in verses 5 and 6 of which chapter it is more fully stated that

"David gathered all Israel together, from Shihor of Egypt even unto the entering of Hemath, to bring the ark of God from Kirjath-jearim.

"And David went up, and all Israel to Baalah, that is to Kirjath-jearim, which belonged to Judah, to bring up thence the ark of God the Lord, that dwelleth between the cherubims whose name is called on it."

The expression " Whose name is called on it," is worthy

of our notice. It is somewhat differently given in 2 Samuel
VI. 2. Here it sounds as though God bestowed such honour
on the ark, that He allowed Himself to be named from it,
the God of the ark, the God who sitteth between the
cherubim upon the ark. Others read the expression thus:
"Whose name is proclaimed;" as though the wonders
which had been wrought by the ark, under Joshua, were
the means of proclaiming the name of the true God among
the surrounding nations. While the expression in the
Chronicles—"Whose name is called *on* it"—is thought to
allude to the solemn pronunciation of the divine name and
titles, by the high priest, on the great day of atonement.

3. Arrived at Kirjath-jearim, which, no doubt, had
received due notice of the arrival, David and all his com-
pany arrange or witness the removal and procession of the
ark. It is reverently placed on a new cart, and drawn—
not by kine—but by oxen. This device seems to have been
borrowed as a hint from the Philistines, which, as it succeeded well with them, might be expected to succeed equally
well with Israel. But, what God may allow among his
enemies, in the absence of properly prescribed means, is
no rule for what He requires of his fully furnished friends.
The Philistines had neither priests of the tabernacle nor
Levites among them. To substitute any of the priests of
Dagon might be feared as an affront to the dreaded ark.
Hence the equipment of a *new cart*, and a couple of untrained kine, was as reasonable a device as any which
could be formed. But with David and Israel the case was
very different. It had been expressly appointed that none
but the Kohathite Levites should carry the ark, and none

but the priests should touch it. The Levites, of course, might touch the staves of the ark, but not the ark itself.— (Numbers IV. 15) How it was that David committed so grievous an oversight, or how it was that no one in Israel thought of it in time to correct it, is left to our conjecture only. On David's part, it shows us that the holiest believers never have too much knowledge of the written word. They may always be increasing their acquaintance with it. It is possible that David's discovery of his singular oversight led him to a closer study of the law of his God, and that, as a consequence of that study, he wrote the long and memorable CXIX. Psalm, in which almost every verse contains some allusion to or some commendation of " the statutes of the Lord." *

4. And, now, the procession, being formed, most jubilantly advances. The two surviving sons of Abinadab, or of Eleazar, for the former, at least, seems to have previously died, assumed, or had granted to them, the honour of seeing to the transit of the ark. Ahio drave the oxen, and Uzzah went behind to steady or otherwise help the cart. " And David and all Israel played before God with all their " might, and with singing, and with harps, and with psal- " teries, and with timbrels, and with cymbals, and with trumpets." † (1 Chronicles XIII. 8.)

* Why it was that the priests and Levites participated in the oversight is more easily accounted for. They had, as a body, totally neglected the ark; and long disuse of the forms prescribed for its locomotion, rendered them really ignorant of them.

† It is singular that such a diligent student of Holy Scripture as Bishop Hall should say—" I did not *before* hear of *trumpets*," as though there had been no trumpets in the procession round Jericho.

Everything proceeded joyously till they came to a particular spot, when, in a moment, all was stopped. The oxen stumbled, or, in some way, shook the cart and the ark in it, (for there is much criticism on the subject), and Uzzah, to prevent, as he thought, damage or mischief, " put forth his hand to hold the ark." In that instant he fell a ghastly corpse. The Lord smote him, but whether with lightning, or some internal rupture, as many think, we are not informed. The shock was terrible to all Israel, and to none more than to David. The singing and playing soon ceased, and the whole march as speedily stopped. The mirth was turned into mourning. Bright faces gathered blackness, and cheerful hearts heaved with dread; for who could tell what sudden blow might next be inflicted, or on whom it might fall? Even David was not without alarm; for " David was afraid of God that day, saying, How shall I bring the ark of God home to me?" Oh, how well is it, and what a good sign rises out of it, when judgments upon others make men begin to tremble for themselves! It is half the work of sanctification accomplished when we are afraid of bringing home to ourselves what has been chastisement and death to others. To think of our own sins when other sinners are cut down in their sins is a good beginning, and one which carries with it much hope.

5. But, *what* was the sin of Uzzah, that it should be followed by a punishment so sudden and so signal? It was *not* an act of wanton sacrilege or wilful contempt, neither was it an intentional wrong of any kind. In fact, Uzzah meant well. He thought to do God service by saving the

ark from a blow or a fall. But, it was not his place to do anything of the kind. It was, therefore, an officious act. It was one which did not pertain to him; for he was, at most, but a Levite, and had no authority to touch the ark on any occasion, or under any pretence whatever. It was, also, a thoughtless act. In fact, the essence of his sin seems to have been irreverence, through a careless and inconsiderate state of mind. He was not, at the time, indulging in high and hallowed reverence for that God over whose ark he was watching. He forgot that, while the cart carried the ark, the ark sustained the presence of Jehovah between the cherubim upon it. The want of due mindfulness of God, especially in those who profess to be patterns of it, is a grievous offence, and an aggravated affront. Besides, as Jewish writers insinuate, Uzzah, by attending on the ark in his father's house, contracted that sort of familiarity with its awful presence which led to an unhallowed demeanour towards it. We are always in danger of the same evil from similar privileges; for the human heart is sadly prone to fall into irreverence, by its habitual association with holy things. Uzzah, too, may have presumed upon his past services to the ark, and so have been tempted of the devil to make a vain display of himself on the occasion. He would appear a great man in the eyes of the multitude to be able to do what none of that multitude dare attempt. Vanity has made victims of many of its votaries.

But, whatever was the real character of Uzzah's crime, the Righteous Lord, against whom it was committed, saw fit to punish it with the instant death of the body. That death is no proof of any perdition of the soul. Uzzah, as a young man, may have been what Eli was as an old man—a true believer—and so have been saved eternally, while he suffered temporally. The punishment was upon one; the fear was upon all. God has perfect right to select his instances of chastisement, as well as his instances of favour.

But, some men will say, " Where is the benevolence and mercy of God in slaying a man for simply touching the ark, and that with a good intention? Can it be wise or expedient to take away life for a single offence, and such an offence as did no injury to any one?" They who question thus know nothing as they ought to know. Their question is next of kin to the infidel question, " Was it fitting to doom Adam and Eve to perdition for eating a single apple?" When we are once correctly informed of the holiness of God, and the lofty majesty of his commands, we shall cease to question thus. We shall see that the divine sanctity cannot endure being infringed upon by the very slightest contact of sin.

6. God's stroke on Uzzah so confounded David, and spread such dismay among the assembled throngs, that the procession was broken up, and every thought of marching further forward that day was laid aside. So unhinged was David by the event, that he fell, for the moment, into infirmity of temper. "David was *displeased*, because the Lord had made a breach upon Uzzah." David had, in consequence, to learn the holy lessons of wisdom and humility; which as the issue proves, he submissively learned. All the Lord's people will have to learn the like, and perhaps

at a sharper cost, when they rashly impugn the divine deal-
ings or indulge in fretful and moody feelings respecting them.

Hard by the spot where Uzzah fell was the house of a
pious Levite—Obed-edom. There David left the ark, till
such time as he could recover himself, and see his way to
further proceedings. Obed-edom, too, was willing to receive
the ark, though everybody on that day was afraid of it,
and even David was unwilling to house it. How are we to
account for this conduct on the part of Obed-edom? On
the principal of true faith and sterling piety it is easily to
be accounted for. "Perfect love casteth out fear:" and
the eye of faith sees the terrors of the Lord laid aside, and
smiles taking their place. Where there is no mind to
transgress, there is no sense of benumbing dread in looking
up to God. Obed-edom knew that there was nothing to
fear from the ark, if he, as a Levite, did only what Levites
might do. Besides, he was not alarmed at the inflictions
of God's justice, since he took refuge in his mercy. Indeed, true piety sees, in the justice of God, not reasons for
servile fear, but grounds for deeper adoration and more
solemn love; as one says, "Even the justice of God is
lovely to the true children of God."

II. *The renewal of David's preparations* followed his devout
reflections upon the solemn event, and his hearing of the extraordinary prosperity which the presence of the ark brought
to the house of Obed-edom. For "The Lord blessed the
house of Obed-edom, and all that he had."—1 Chron. XIII.
14. The Jews report the most extravagant things of the
blessedness which crowned his family and his property.*

* They say that he was blessed with extraordinary health after

Though their reports may be fabulously exaggerated, yet, without doubt, the personal and domestic prosperity of the good man was very great. So true is it that "Godliness is great gain," and that "the blessing of the Lord it maketh rich, and He addeth no sorrow unto it." Oh, therefore, that men would seek to have God always with them, and that they would believe in the sure prosperity which his presence always brings.

1. And, now, David begins his renewal of pains to bring up the ark to Jerusalem, by an ingenuous acknowledgement of his error about the cart and the oxen on the former occasion. "Then David said, none ought to carry the ark of God but the Levites."—(1 Chronicles xv. 2.) We can never set about a renewal of efforts, after some signal failure, more hopefully than by candidly confessing to ourselves and to others the weak or deficient points in our former efforts. With a conviction of his error in his own mind, David openly avowed it to those who were chiefly concerned to repair it.—1 Chronicles xv. 11, 12, 13.*

sickness and a singular influx of wealth. This is not unlikely: but when they say that he had eight married sons, and that the wife of each son bore eight children at a birth, and that within *three* months, (!) they talk as Jewish writers too often talk.

* "And David called for Zadok and Abiathar the priests, and for the Levites, for Uriel, Asaiah, and Joel, Shemaiah and Eliel, and Amminadab,

"And said unto them, Ye are the chief of the fathers of the Levites: Sanctify yourselves, both ye and your brethren, that ye may bring up the ark of the Lord God of Israel unto the place that I have prepared for it.

"For because ye did it not at the first, the Lord our God made a breach upon us, for that we sought him not after due order."

After this, David made at once an orderly and very extensive arrangement for the procession of the ark from the house of Obed-edom to the tent, which he had pitched for it, in Jerusalem. The whole staff of priests and Levites, soldiers and elders, singers and instrumental musicians, seem to have been engaged for the occasion. It was thus arranged, because David intended to make the procession as splendid and as joyous as he possibly could. That nothing might be wanting in its hallowed hilarity, himself headed the procession, not in royal state, but habited as a sort of lay-priest,* wearing a linen ephod, or short white surplice, in order to show that he was more anxious to be a believer than a king, and to impress on his subjects the conviction that all he did in bringing up the ark was of a religious rather than of a civil character.

2. Setting out on their homeward course, David was mindful of what he had before omitted. He provided for the offering of sacrifices to Almighty God. (2 Samuel VI. 13.) This was the sure way to arrive at a successful issue. May we always prove it so to be! Now that the procession was in full progress, David was to be seen "dancing and playing with all his might." Some kind of harp employed his hands, while his feet were occupied in musical paces, and keeping time to the tune, as well as to the graceful and ecstatic motions of his whole person. The dance of David was wholly of a religious character, and consequently

---

* Our Henry the Eighth, in the earlier part of his reign, occasionally did the like, in private service. And Sir Thomas Moore often put on a surplice in the chapel at Kensington and took part with the choir.

marked with sobriety and devotion as well as with fervour and animation. It accorded with the age of the church and the custom of the times. The Holy Ghost at once sanctified and sanctioned it.*

But, it is seldom that an earnest believer escapes censure or contempt for his earnestness. Saul's daughter, who was now David's wife, but who retained too much of the temper of her father, looked out of a window as the ark was passing through Jerusalem, and, seeing her husband dancing and playing, "despised him in her heart." Well, perhaps, would it have been had she kept her feelings within her heart. But, in a fit of ill and contemptuous temper, she told her mind to David. Her quarrel with him was of her own making. God took it up against herself, and pronounced upon her a sentence, than which nothing could be more vexatious to a Hebrew wife, namely, that she should for ever be childless.

3. It has pleased the Holy Ghost to leave on record two, at least, of the divine songs which David composed for the procession of the ark to his city and home. The XXIV. and LXVIII. are those songs or psalms. The LXVIII. Psalm was probably sung while the ark was on the road to Jerusalem, and the XXIV. when it reached the tent of its residence. The first verse and the last of the LXVIII. are peculiarly descriptive of the circumstances under which the ark was carried to Jerusalem. "Let God arise and let his enemies be scattered," were words which carried back the hearers

* That religious dances were practised in christian churches during "the dark ages" is notorious. In some of the Spanish Cathedrals even Bishops have headed them.

to the days of the ark in the wilderness, when, upon its going forward, Moses said, "Rise up Lord, and let thine enemies be scattered!" while the last verse, "O God, thou art terrible out of thy holy places!" seems plainly to allude to the fearful death of Uzzah upon the former attempt to remove the ark. The xxiv Psalm is beautifully prophetic of the Ascension of Christ to heaven, from the figure of the ark ascending the holy hill of Zion. When all was ended, as to its safe deposit on that hill, David offered abundant sacrifices, liberally regaled the people, and dismissed them with his fervent blessing. Thus, while he acted as a godly man and a generous prince, he was displayed by God as an eminent type of the Messiah conducting his people to the true Jerusalem, accepting their thanksgivings, and regaling and blessing them in their everlasting home.

It remains for us to contemplate

III. *The elevation of the ark by Solomon to its grand and final resting place in the temple.*

David never intended the tent, which he pitched for it, to be its ultimate abode. A loftier device had entered his mind. He commended that device to his God, who approved it, but directed its accomplishment to be postponed to the days of his son and successor. David's hands had been too much stained with the blood of war to render him a ritually fit person to erect a temple for peaceful worship. Still, he was allowed to communicate the plan of that temple, and to make the most lavish preparation of materials for it. In due time, Solomon applied all the vast resources of both his mind and his wealth to the completion of his father's plan.

1. When the temple was finished, the young king, like his father, made sumptuous and splendid arrangements for conveying "the ark of the covenant" from the tent on Zion to the holy of holies on Moriah. He assembled all the principal men of his empire, and took care that everything should be conducted in due order. He learned what to do from the painful lessons which his royal father had learned before him. Sacrifices innumerable were offered; and priests were the bearers of the ark to the hallowed place appointed for it. The procession must have been eminently gorgeous and grand, and yet intensely solemn and devout. The full account is recorded in 2 Chronicles v. 2—8. In the last two verses it is said—

"And the priests brought in the ark of the covenant of the Lord unto his holy place, to the oracle of the house, into the most holy place, even under the wings of the cherubims:

"For the cherubims spread forth their wings over the ark, and the cherubims covered the ark and the staves thereof above."

This addition of gigantic cherubim to shadow not only the other cherubim on the ark, but the whole area of the holy of holies, was a magnificent device, full of significance to those who look to the heaven of heavens as filled with all the fulness of divine and angelic beauty.

2. While marching from the tent to the temple, the singers were, no doubt, suitably employed. Whether they repeated the Psalms which David composed for the former occasion, we cannot say; but it is currently believed that Psalms XLVII. and CXXXII. were used for this last procession, and that each was written by Solomon, or some other inspired person, for that special solemnity.

3. As Solomon made the elevation of the ark to its resting place the first thing in all that he devised for that glorious day, which many believe to have been the chief day of a year of Jubilee, so was it the last thing at which he glanced in the noble and magnificent dedication prayer which he addressed to the God of Israel.

"Now therefore arise, O Lord God, unto thy resting place, thou and the ark of thy strength : let thy priests, O Lord God, be clothed with thy salvation, and let thy saints rejoice in goodness."

Solomon well knew that, as the temple was nothing without the ark, so was the ark nothing without the presence of the eternal God. With it, therefore, he prayed that Jehovah would condescend to come, and make the holy of holies his "resting place." Jehovah heard the prayer, and allowed the ark to continue as the focus of his presence, for many a generation. The rest which the ark began to have when David lodged it in Jerusalem, was continued in a special manner during the whole of Solomon's reign, "for his God gave him rest round about." No enemy assailed the tent of David, or the temple of Solomon, and no war called forth the ark into a field of battle. Sweet and beautiful emblem this of the repose of Christ after the sufferings of his manhood, and his ascension to the true temple above. When He ascended up on high, it was to enter into his rest; for He had been a man of labours and sorrows on earth. There, as the True Ark, He remains, never again to be personally smitten and afflicted, never again to be taken captive, by wicked men, more cruel than Philistines, and never needing rescue, temporary sojourn, or another ascension. For ever and for ever shall his rest be glorious.

As we have now travelled through the history of the ark till it has reached its topmost elevation, let us tarry a while to glance at a few prominent points, which the retrospect presents to us.

1. It may be that the main divisions of the history of the ark in Canaan *were intended to foreshadow the main divisions of the gospel dispensation.* If so, we have fresh cause to take comfort in our prospects.

The prosperity of the ark under Joshua, and during the age of those who immediately succeeded him, seems to meet with its counterpart, in the prosperity of genuine truth, from the ministry of our Lord to the death of his apostles and their immediate successors. After Joshua and his companions left the world, an entirely different class of Jews speedily sprung up. "There arose another generation after them which knew not the Lord."—Judges II. 10. So, after the apostolic age men of other minds soon spread over the church, and another gospel crept in. Checks and alternations of light and darkness occurred in Israel, till at length the mass of the priesthood was a mass of corruption, and the ark was separated from the tabernacle. So, with many undulations, the pure truth of Christ sank into obscurity under the darkness of the so-called dark ages ; the gospel seemed to be separated from the visible church, and cold indifference generally prevailed. But, there came a great reformation in Israel under David : the ark was restored, and a new era in a new part of the land set in. So our European Reformation restored the gospel, and set forth Christ as the Ark of the new covenant. But, then, that Ark was sent, not to Italy, but chiefly to England. To England all eyes now look as the most favoured spot in the world, and which may prove another Jerusalem, or focus for the outspreading of the light of a millennium, which will answer to the glories of the reign of Solomon.

Be the result as it may, let us watch and wait for the exaltation of that Saviour who is the only glory of his people.

2. The perfect singularity, pre-eminence, and isolation of the ark, should remind us of *the grand peculiarity, which, in every point of view, pertains to Christ.* There was but one ark; everything was formed for it; and, without it, nothing in Israel had life or prosperity. God has studied the like peculiarity with regard to his dear Son. Him, and Him alone, has He set before the eye of his church. All through its ages and its history He is to be the one concentrated object of desire. His presence is everything, and without it we shall in vain look for vitality or blessedness. —Acts IV. 12. Oh that all who call themselves christians did but steadfastly hold to the pre-eminence of Christ! Were He, in the estimation of his professed followers, what He is in Himself, " the first and the last," the " all-in-all," there would be neither Popery, feeble Protestantism, sect nor schism, within the pale of the visible church. When Israel held to the ark, and gloried in it alone, there was neither false God among them, nor war to trouble them. Our state will correspond with theirs, when Christ alone is exalted among us.

3. In tracing the ark to its long-intended resting place, we may discern *the joyful certainty of all God's purposes.* Many a time did it seem to go ill with the ark, and the

prospect of its ultimate glory appeared most dim and uncertain. But the glorious end was attained. So, when Christ on the Cross, like the ark in Dagon's temple, was given over for lost, who felt confident of the glory which was to follow? Yet the glory did follow. So, many a time does the humble christian seem to himself ready to perish; but, relief comes in due season, and assuredly God will bring him to where his Saviour is. He shall attain the end of his faith, even the salvation of his soul.

LECTURE VI.

"And the temple of God was opened in heaven, and there was seen in his temple the ark of his testament."—Rev. xi. 19.

WE hear, in these words, the last mention of the ark in Holy Scripture. But, ere we come to the contemplation of them, we must trace our path through a few other texts, which occur subsequently to those days of Solomon with which our last lecture concluded. For the completion of the plan of these lectures, we have now, finally, to consider "The History of the Ark from the reign of Solomon to the latest mention of it in Holy Scripture." May, then, this last attempt to elucidate an interesting and important topic of divine revelation, be not the least in point of spiritual profit and hallowed pleasure.

I. For full four hundred years we find no mention of the ark in the record of the kings of Judah. True, the ark was to *rest* in the temple; but the exercise of men's affections towards it was to be constant and energetic. It was not to be brought from its place in the holy of holies; neither did any one, except the high priest, and that once a year only, dare to go in to gaze upon it. In this respect it was a notable type of the Invisible One, whom, though not seen, the people were to believe, reverence, and love.

During the days of Solomon all was peaceful and prosperous with Israel. The memorable wonders of the dedication of the temple, and the splendid procession which brought up "the ark of the covenant" into it, lived in the mental eye of many a true worshipper of the God of Israel.

In the reign of his son and successor, Rehoboam, the ark, indeed, continued in its rest, but the first interruptions of that rest were felt, in the dismemberment of the kingdom, and in the establishment of a spurious form of worship for ten out of the twelve tribes. Rehoboam was an unwise ruler, and far more despotically disposed than either justice or prudence required. Taking advantage of this, Jeroboam the son of Nebat was permitted to organize a revolution, which shook the pillars of the empire to their lowest basement. The one nation separated into two kingdoms. Israel mustered ten tribes, and Judah comprised only two. But, then, Judah retained the temple and the ark of the covenant. Jeroboam was too shrewd a man not to perceive the immense advantage which this gave to Judah, and the necessity for devising some substitute for what the people had been accustomed to regard as essential to their security and prosperity. He, accordingly, set up a sort of counterfeit ark, or at least, that sort of imitation of the cherubic figures upon it, which would best engage the thoughts of the people, and satisfy his own idolatrous inclinations. He made "a house of high places," and instituted services and sacrifices after a distorted fashion, so as to beguile the people into the belief that their attendance on them would excuse their going to Jerusalem. But, as the people were familiar with the form of the cherubim, he made and set up " two golden calves," and said, " Behold thy Gods, O Israel !" Now, we are not to suppose that these golden calves were mere likenesses of the animal which we well know by that name, or that the people were, all at once, so befooled and besotted as to worship such creatures. Had they so been, it would have better served their purpose to select a living calf at a far less cost, than to make a golden one. But this was quite foreign to Jeroboam's policy. The cherubim on the ark were made of gold, and as the calves were partial imitations of them, it was expedient for these calves, also, to be formed of gold.

Possibly, however, you are startled at the idea of there being anything cherubic in the calves of Jeroboam. The surprise will cease when you recollect that the first face of the cherubim was that of an ox, and that the feet of the whole were those of a calf. The common figure, too, of a cherub was ox-like, with wings. " He rode on a cherub (a winged ox) and did fly ; yea, He did fly upon the wings of the wind." (Ps. XVIII. 10.) Modern discoveries among the buried ruins of Nineveh, have brought to light " the winged bull " of the Assyrian religion, which, like the Apis, or symbolic calf of Egypt, with many another similar device, was, no doubt, a distortion of the patriarchial knowledge of the form of the cherubim, as first displayed at the gate of the Edenic Paradise.

Thus, Jeroboam's counterfeit of the figures on the mercy-seat of the ark, was not so much the substitution of pagan idolatry, as of a spurious form of true Judaism. It was the popery of its day, being a corruption of Jehovah's religion, and in reality antagonistic to it.

But, how came it that such an imposture was so easily palmed upon the people? Jewish historians tell many tales to account for it, but they fail in giving the true reason. It was not the eloquence or cunning of Jeroboam in first winning over the chiefs of the tribes; but it was the hollow-heartedness of the people themselves. Unless they had themselves turned away, in heart, from the God of the ark, they would not so soon and so easily have been turned by Jeroboam to worship his golden calves. All apostacy, like all true religion, begins in the heart. When the inner man is unsound, the outer life will be unfaithful. Israel ceased to love God before they began to love idols. So, to this hour, they who once appeared sound in the faith, but have turned aside to worldly folly, popery, or infidelity, have first turned from the love of truth and holiness in their hearts.

II. In the history of the ark, time leads us on to the beginning of the reign of the young but good Josiah. We read nothing respecting the ark during the many reigns which preceded his. And, yet, there must have been many occurrences which affected it; especially in the reigns of those wicked princes who suffered the temple to fall into decay, and who loved idols more than the ark. How it was preserved during the atrocious usurpation of Athaliah, or what was done with it when Jehoash, under the counsel of the good priest Jehoida, extensively repaired the house of the Lord we are not informed. Neither know we how it fared when the wicked Ahaz,* the father of the

* Why Ahaz spared the ark, when he "gathered together the

righteous Hezekiah, perverted every ordinance of God, despoiled the temple, and turned the whole tide of the national religion into heathenism. Neither, again, do we hear anything of it, even when Hezekiah set about a thorough reformation, and restored all the services of the sanctuary. In fact, it is not till the rise of his great grandson, Josiah, (as already stated,) that we find any mention of the ark at all. But, then, that mention of it helps us to understand somewhat of its previous history. The record is found, not in the Book of Kings, but in 2 Chron. xxxv. 3.

From the wording of this text, we are led to infer that, during the abominable life of Manasseh, and the short but wicked reign of his son Amon, there were some truly pious Levites, holy and devoted men of heart, who had removed and taken care of the ark. It is probable, therefore, that when they saw the horrible impiety of Manasseh, how, amongst other things, "he set a carved image (the idol which he had made) in the house of God," and built idolatrous altars actually within that holy house, that they, most likely at the risk of their lives, secured the ark by carrying it away into the country, and lodging it, as occasion served, in the house of some true-hearted Israelite, who, like

vessels of the house of God, and cut them in pieces," (2 Chron. xxviii. 24,) can only be accounted for by supposing that secret fear of consequences restrained him. He could not be ignorant of the terrible power of the ark in former days, and how Uzzah fell down dead for merely touching it. Some such reason as this, perhaps, prevented invading armies from capturing and carrying it off, till, at length, the visible token of Jehovah's presence (the Shekinah) was withdrawn from it.

Abinadab or Obed-edom, was glad to receive it. It is probable, also, that in order to escape detection, they many times were obliged, reverently to convey the ark from place to place, so that, in the words of Josiah, it seemed to be "a burden upon their shoulders." Most likely, also, they acted under the sanction and direction of the high priest of the day, that good man Hilkiah.

How exact a picture, alas, was this of the need of flight and secretion which befel the True Ark, even the Lord Jesus, when to escape the Manasseh of his day—Herod the wickedly great—He was carried into Egypt, and, frequently afterwards, was obliged to hide Himself, or convey Himself away from the grasp of those who sought his life! How painfully, too, has the picture been copied in the lives of the followers of Jesus, "who wandered about in sheep-skins and goat-skins (the ark, when travelling, was covered with badger-skins) being destitute, afflicted, tormented!" May we be spared from witnessing the same sort of wanderings, and enduring the like afflictions!

The ark, once again restored to its rightful place in the holy of holies, had a short rest, during the reign of Josiah. But, that rest was only like the brief lull of a tempest which is about to desolate every spot within its range. The time for the total loss of the ark, or, at least, for its historic annihilation, was rapidly coming on. The measure of the national iniquity was fast filling up, and God was about to give up his vineyard to the wild boar of the wood. But, ere the threatened vengeance is dashed upon the people, their city and their temple, the sweet voice of prophecy is heard, tuning its gentlest strain to a song of future times. To this prophetic song we must now turn our attentive ear.

III. The prophet Jeremiah lived in the reign of Josiah. He saw its beginning and its end. He, consequently, saw the good things which Josiah did; and, among them, the desired restoration of the ark to the renovated temple. This must have been a joy to such a man as Jeremiah. But, much as he may have rejoiced at this time, the Spirit of Prophecy carried him forward to another time, even to the full day of Christ on earth, when neither the temple nor the ark should be objects of desire, because of the knowledge and presence of Him who is greater than both. Thus speaks the prophecy:

"And it shall come to pass, when ye be multiplied and increased in the land, in those days, saith the Lord, they shall say no more, The ark of the covenant of the Lord: neither shall it come to mind; neither shall they remember it; neither shall they visit it; neither shall that be done any more.

"At that time they shall call Jerusalem the throne of the Lord; and all nations shall be gathered unto it, to the name of the Lord, to Jerusalem: neither shall they walk any more after the imagination of their evil heart."—Jeremiah iii. 16, 17.

There are some biblical students, who, viewing distant events with a too considerably shortened telescope, interpret this prophecy as already fulfilled. They imagine that it was fulfilled when, after the captivity in Babylon, the people returned to Judea, re-built the temple, without the ark, and increased and multiplied both in population and prosperity. But, assuredly, in that return to Judea there was nothing like the accomplishment of the many glorious things which Jeremiah foretold, when he spake of the people neither having the ark, nor longing for it. Besides, the broad and palpable fact is, that the Jewish nation did long for the ark, and the other things which, together with it, were missing in the second temple, and for all of which they do long and sigh to the present day. In many of their synagogues they have a holy chest or coffer, in which they keep manuscript copies of the Old Testament, on rolls of vellum or parchment, and which they take out, unfold, and read with great solemnity on special occasions. Without doubt, as the good and the wise, in overwhelming majority, think, the times to which the words of Jeremiah refer are the times of Messiah in his millennial glory. Then the gathered and honoured Jews, having Him for their Saviour and King, and being made altogether a spiritually minded people, shall no longer care for any figure or shadow of Him, such as their ark and other ceremonial forms had presented to their fore-fathers. Oh, happy day, and happy they who see it, when the long-predicted glory of Israel shall fill the earth, and all nations shall flow unto it.

But, we must go back to the dark day of Israel's banishment from the inheritance of Canaan.

IV. After ages of fruitless trial, and unfelt forbearance, Jehovah let his justice take its course. The process, both of the mercy shewn to Israel and of the judgment which terminated it, is thus affectingly described in 2 Chron. XXXVI. 15—19.—

"And the Lord of their fathers sent to them by his messengers, rising up betimes and sending; because he had compassion on his people, and on his dwelling place.

"But they mocked the messengers of God and despised his words, and misused his prophets, until the wrath of the Lord arose against his people, till there was no remedy.

"Therefore he brought upon them the king of the Chaldeans, who slew their young men with the sword in the house of their sanctuary, and had no compassion upon young man or maiden, old man or him that stooped for age, he gave them all into his hand.

"And all the vessels of the house of God, great and small, and the treasures of the house of the Lord, and the treasures of the king and of his princes, all these he brought to Babylon.

And they burnt the house of God, and brake down the wall of Jerusalem, and burnt all the palaces thereof with fire, and destroyed all the goodly vessels thereof."

In 2 Kings, xxv. 13—17, a minuter account is given of the spoils of the temple. But in this particular account no mention is made of the ark. All that Nebuchadnezzar took from the temple he carried to Babylon. The meaner spoil of brass he seems to have broken up and used: but all the more valuable articles he deposited in the house of his idol-god. There they continued, apparently catalogued with great exactness, till Cyrus gained possession of them, when he conquered the kingdom. Upon his being divinely moved to let the Hebrews return to their country, he generously gave them back all the gold and silver vessels, amounting to five thousand and four hundred. Still, though many articles are expressly named, no allusion to the ark is made. (See Ezra i. 7—11.) Hence the question very naturally presents itself, What became of the ark, and what was its ultimate lot? This is answered in two or three ways. 1. By some persons it is thought that the ark was not carried to Babylon at all, but that, in like manner as it was secreted by some pious Levites, in the dark reign of Manasseh, so was it secured and privately conveyed away by some equally pious individuals, when the Babylonian storm was seen to be approaching. In this case, it is further supposed, that the ark was concealed in some cave, or covered recess, on lofty hill or in sequestered dale, and that, being of imperishable materials, it remains there to this day, preserved for happy discovery in some bright hour of Israel's joy. 2. Others are of opinion that the ark *was* carried to Babylon, but that, having been in some untold way disposed of, it was not returned to Jerusalem. They even imagine that it may still be extant among the ruins of the temples or treasuries of Babylon, and that, to answer some important object in the day of Israel's controversy, it will be brought to light. 3. Others, again, settle it in their minds that the ark was both carried to Babylon and returned to Jerusalem: for, say they, its not being named among the articles which were taken and then given back, is a thing of no force, because other articles of the larger sort, are, also, not named.

Among our English divines, the principal advocate of this last opinion is Dr. Prideaux, in his well-known work on the Connexion between the Old and the New Testament. In discussing the question whether the second temple had or had not " the ark of the covenant," he takes the affirmative side. His argument is to this effect: that as the holy of holies, and the vail before it, in the first temple, were for containing and concealing the ark, and as the second temple had both a holy of holies and a vail, so, also, it must have had either *the* ark or *one made anew* in resemblance of it. And, further, that as the high priest continued to go, once a year, to sprinkle the blood of atonement in the holy of holies, so there must have been an ark, if not *the* ark before which to sprinkle it.

In reply to this reasoning, it is urged that the Jews universally assert that there was no ark in the second temple, for it was one of the five things which that temple wanted, in comparison with the first temple. They, also, assert that, in lieu of the ark, there was set in the holy of holies of the second temple a large stone, which was dug up from the ruins of the first temple, and supposed to be its foundation, or chief corner-stone.

With this opinion, as to the absence of the ark from the second temple, nearly all the early Christian writers agree. Josephus, also, states that the ark was wanting in it; and that, when Titus, the commander of the Roman forces, captured Jerusalem, and went into the holy of holies, no ark was seen within it.

In corroboration of this opinion, perhaps the following fact, as a new argument, may be admitted: There stands at Rome, to this day, a triumphal arch, "The Arch of Titus," commemorative of the victory of that illustrious general over the Jews and Jerusalem. Within it are sculptured the forms of several of the vessels of the sanctuary, but there is no representation of the ark. Now, it is hardly to be imagined that a Roman artist, in designing such an arch, would have omitted the chief symbol of the Jewish worship, and have selected only secondary objects, if the ark had been known to be among the spoils of the temple.*

* Neither the Coliseum nor the greater part of the monuments now

With the generality therefore, of historians and divines, we may pretty safely conclude that the ark was unknown to the worshippers in the second temple. But, what really became of it after the desolation of the first temple, no man can tell.

We have, however, an authentic revelation respecting Christ as the True Ark, in the vision of St. John, whose words we have now to consider.

V. In our text, the favoured Apostle writes that " the " temple of God was opened in heaven, and there was seen " in his temple the ark of his testament."

The general meaning of this statement in the Apocalyptic vision, is that at the period referred to, though that period is differently interpreted, there should be an enlarged

seen from the Capitol, were erected till after St. Paul's death. Of these there is one which, to the Christian or the Jew, must ever be the most interesting at Rome, marking as it does, the final downfall of the Jewish state, and preserving upon its triumphal tablets the only authentic representation in existence of the implements of the temple worship. This is the Arch of Titus, erected, after his death, to commemmorate his capture of Jerusalem, and which is, perhaps, the most simple and beautiful at Rome. The ruined frieze bears the triumphal procession of the conqueror, and sculptured on the wall, *within* the archway, is a procession of captive Jews, bearing on their shoulders the spoils of the temple at Jerusalem, the eleven-branched golden candlestick, the jubilee trumpets, the tables of *the* shew bread, and other details copied, no doubt, from the originals themselves, which, deposited in the temples, are said to have been finally carried away by Genseric into Africa. This sculptured tablet, and the edifice which it adorns, form, perhaps, the most vivid page in monumental history, to be met with in the whole world."—*From Bartlett's Footsteps of our Lord and his Apostles.*

H

opening for the spread of true religion, and a clearer discovery
of the mystery of Christ. The ark was not seen when it
stood in the temple, but was concealed by a veil. As that
ark was the symbol of the person and the presence of Christ,
so, the throwing of it open, the causing of it to be seen by
all eyes, was a mode of stating that the time should come
when the mystery of the Gospel of Christ should be more
clearly developed, and the distinctive doctrines of Christianity more plainly and forcibly presented to the people.
Whether the time intended by the vision referred to the
time of the Great Reformation, or, as some think, to the
present times, as the continuance of that revival of true
evangelical doctrine which has marked the present century,
we profess not to determine. Be this as it may, we know,
from the text, that "the ark of the covenant" was certainly
a type of Christ. And, happy, too, is the knowledge that
his doctrine is more fully and more faithfully preached in
the pulpits of our land, and more extensively promulgated
through the world than in any former age. May it not be
that another verse or two in this wonderful revelation, apparently co-significant with our text, has yet to be fulfilled.
In Rev. xv. 5—8, it is said,

"And after that I looked, and, behold, the temple of the tabernacle
of the testimony in heaven was opened.

"And the seven angels came out of the temple, having the seven
plagues, clothed in pure and white linen, and having their breasts
girded with golden girdles.

"And one of the four beasts gave unto the seven angels seven golden
vials full of the wrath of God, who liveth for ever and ever.

"And the temple was filled with smoke from the glory of God, and
from his power: and no man was able to enter into the temple, till the
seven plagues of the seven angels were fulfilled."

This filling of the temple with smoke, and the inability of men to enter into it, is thought to mean the mist which will envelope the Church through Anti-christian teaching, and which will prevent souls from entering into the true temple, till after the threatened plagues upon the enemies of Christ shall be accomplished. We know what that mist is doing now. The good Lord deliver us and all ours from its deathly gloom, and keep us in the true light of his dear Son. Sure may we be that, when God manifests the truth to us, it is that we may clearly discern it, and affectionately receive it. To our view "the ark of his testament" has been disclosed. The veil which for ages intercepted our sight of its glories has long been withdrawn. Opportunities for stedfastly gazing upon it and contemplating it in all its wondrous proportions, are amply furnished to us. May our diligence, our earnestness, our gratitude, be commensurate with our privileges! And may the illustrations of the subject which have been presented in these lectures, be one means, at least, of enhancing our estimate of those privileges. Let none forget that, if they regard them only as intellectually pleasant, they dishonour their intention and fail to realize them as spiritually profitable.

Let your renewed attention accompany our winding up of the present lecture, as the last of the series.

1. In the policy of Jeroboam to substitute golden calves for "the ark of the covenant," and thereby to content the people with a counterfeit religion, let us behold *a type of the great apostacy in the Christian Israel, and beware of it*. The one was, doubtless, intended to foreshadow the other: for, as under the Old Dispensation, there was a great falling

away of the majority of the tribes from the worship of the true God, so was there to be a similar defection under the new. For it is written, "that day (the day of the Lord) shall not come except there come a falling away (or a great apostacy) first." That falling away has long been grievously visible in Christendom. The proportion of the spurious to the sound is still as it were, ten to two. Antichrist can boast, like Jeroboam, of numbers. The flock of Christ is still a little flock, but, then, like Judah, they have the True Ark, and as long so they cherish it they shall prosper. In the days of Jeroboam, multitudes of priests, Levites, and people, who loved the ark at Jerusalem, refused to worship the calves, but went and dwelt in Judah. Multitudes, thank God, have left and still are leaving the Church of Rome. To those who stay behind we are with earnest affection to say, "Come out of her, my people, that ye be not partakers of her sins, and that ye receive not of her plagues." (Rev. XVIII. 4.)

Let us hold fast the doctrine of Christ, and never be slack in standing up valiantly for its defence. So long as the ark of God is with us, and we sincerely love it, so long, like Judah, shall we, our Queen and our country, stand and prosper.

2. In the total loss of the ark, and in the entire demolition of the Jewish system, let us discern *the low estimate which God sets upon his own most exalted institutions, in comparison with the living realties, which they were intended to foreshadow.*

The Jewish system of type and ceremony was formed with infinite pains, and at a cost of wisdom and forethought which seemed to draw largely on the divine treasury. It employed the loftiest angels, and the holiest men. It was attended with the most astonishing miracles, and marked the destinies of the world for many ages. All this vast fabric, however, of figurative worship, was accounted nothing in comparison with the simple faith of the simplest believer in the Incarnate Son. When the time for his incarnation was drawing nigh, indications were given of the departure of the types of it. The ark was dislodged from its resting place ; and, after a short restoration, was lost to all human observation. Intimation was hereby given that the True Ark was about to appear, that men were to prepare themselves for its appearance, and that all hearts should be ready to welcome it. Yes, nothing is of any value in God's reckoning apart from his beloved Son. Everything gives place to Him. The curious tabernacle was nothing; the gorgeous temple was nothing; and even the wondrous and glorious ark was nothing ; for they all were consigned to destruction or oblivion. But the Babe of Bethlehem is everything. He is "all and in all"—unchangeable and eternal. Oh, happy experience, to be a penitent believer in Jesus ! He is the Tabernacle which will never decay— the Temple which will never be destroyed—the Ark which will never be lost. All, too, who are found in Him will be what He is. May we be so found !

3. In the visions of St. John, as set forth in our text, *let us see our duty and our joy.* Is the holy of holies thrown open to our view, and the ark of Jehovah's testimony disclosed to us? Let us, then, strive to enter into the one, and never take our eye from the other. The way is

laid open by the flesh of Christ; and, by faith, his people walk in it up to the very ark of their salvation. If, in our day, the mists of anti-christianity should thicken around us, and the darkness of the divine judgments appal our hearts, let us take courage in knowing that "the time is short." Terrible as the judgment will be, it will annihilate every foe, and He, whom our souls love, will be alone exalted, according to the force of that covenant which was made before the world began.

G. WILLIAMS AND CO., PRINTERS, WOLVERHAMPTON.

www.ingramcontent.com/pod-product-compliance
Lightning Source LLC
LaVergne TN
LVHW061219060426
835508LV00014B/1357